James Stuart Candlish

The work of the Holy Spirit

James Stuart Candlish

The work of the Holy Spirit

ISBN/EAN: 9783337282929

Printed in Europe, USA, Canada, Australia, Japan

Cover: Foto ©Lupo / pixelio.de

More available books at **www.hansebooks.com**

Handbooks for Bible Classes and Private Students.

EDITED BY
REV. MARCUS DODS, D.D.,
AND
REV. ALEXANDER WHYTE, D.D.

NOW READY.

THE EPISTLE TO THE GALATIANS. By James Macgregor, D.D., late of New College, Edinburgh. *Price 1s. 6d.*

THE POST-EXILIAN PROPHETS. With Introductions and Notes. By Rev. Marcus Dods, D.D., Glasgow. *Price 2s.*

A LIFE OF CHRIST. By Rev. James Stalker, M.A. *Price 1s. 6d.*

THE SACRAMENTS. By Rev. Professor Candlish, D.D. *Price 1s. 6d.*

THE BOOKS OF CHRONICLES. By Rev. Professor Murphy, LL.D., Belfast. *Price 1s. 6d.*

THE CONFESSION OF FAITH. By Rev. John Macpherson, M.A., Findhorn. *Price 2s.*

THE BOOK OF JUDGES. By Rev. Principal Douglas, D.D. *Price 1s. 3d.*

THE BOOK OF JOSHUA. By Rev. Principal Douglas, D.D. *Price 1s. 6d.*

THE EPISTLE TO THE HEBREWS. By Rev. Professor Davidson, D.D., Edinburgh. *Price 2s. 6d.*

SCOTTISH CHURCH HISTORY. By Rev. N. L. Walker. *Price 1s. 6d.*

THE CHURCH. By Rev. Prof. Binnie, D.D., Aberdeen. *Price 1s. 6d.*

THE REFORMATION. By Rev. Professor Lindsay, D.D. *Price 2s.*

THE BOOK OF GENESIS. By Rev. Marcus Dods, D.D. *Price 2s.*

THE EPISTLE TO THE ROMANS. By Rev. Principal Brown, D.D., Aberdeen. *Price 2s.*

PRESBYTERIANISM. By Rev. John Macpherson, M.A. *Price 1s. 6d.*

LESSONS ON THE LIFE OF CHRIST. By Rev. Wm. Scrymgeour, Glasgow. *Price 2s. 6d.*

THE SHORTER CATECHISM. By Rev. Alexander Whyte, D.D., Edinburgh. *Price 2s. 6d.*

[Continued on next page.

HANDBOOKS FOR BIBLE CLASSES.

THE GOSPEL ACCORDING TO ST. MARK. By Rev. Professor LINDSAY, D.D., Glasgow. *Price 2s. 6d.*

A SHORT HISTORY OF CHRISTIAN MISSIONS. By GEORGE SMITH, LL.D., F.R.G.S. *Price 2s. 6d.*

A LIFE OF ST. PAUL. By Rev. JAMES STALKER, M.A. *Price 1s. 6d.*

PALESTINE. With Maps. By Rev. ARCH. HENDERSON, M.A., Crieff. *Price 2s. 6d.*

THE BOOK OF ACTS. By Rev. Professor LINDSAY, D.D. Part I., Chaps. i. to xii. *Price 1s. 6d.* — Part II., Chaps. xiii. to end. *Price 1s. 6d.*

THE WORK OF THE HOLY SPIRIT. By Rev. Professor CANDLISH, D.D. *Price 1s. 6d.*

IN PREPARATION.

THE SUM OF SAVING KNOWLEDGE. By Rev. JOHN MACPHERSON, M.A., Findhorn. *[In the Press.*

THE SABBATH. By Rev. Professor SALMOND, D.D., Aberdeen.

THE GOSPEL ACCORDING TO ST. JOHN. By Rev. GEORGE REITH, M.A., Glasgow. *[Shortly.*

THE FIRST EPISTLE TO THE CORINTHIANS. By Rev. MARCUS DODS, D.D., Glasgow.

THE EPISTLE TO THE PHILIPPIANS. By Rev. JAMES MELLIS, M.A., Southport.

THE EPISTLE TO THE COLOSSIANS. By Rev. SIMEON R. MACPHAIL, M.A., Liverpool.

CHURCH AND STATE. By A. TAYLOR INNES, Esq., Advocate, Edinburgh.

CHRISTIAN ETHICS. By Rev. Professor LINDSAY, D.D., Glasgow.

APOLOGETICS. By Rev. JAMES IVERACH, M.A., Aberdeen.

THE BOOK OF EXODUS. By JAMES MACGREGOR, D.D., late of New College, Edinburgh.

THE DOCTRINE OF SIN. By Rev. Professor CANDLISH, D.D.

ISAIAH. By Rev. Professor EMSLIE M.A., London.

HANDBOOKS

FOR

BIBLE CLASSES

AND PRIVATE STUDENTS.

EDITED BY

REV. MARCUS DODS, D.D.,

AND

REV. ALEXANDER WHYTE, D.D.

CANDLISH ON THE WORK OF THE HOLY SPIRIT.

EDINBURGH:
T. & T. CLARK, 38 GEORGE STREET.

PRINTED BY MORRISON AND GIBB,

FOR

T. & T. CLARK, EDINBURGH.

LONDON,	HAMILTON, ADAMS, AND CO.
DUBLIN,	GEORGE HERBERT.
NEW YORK,	SCRIBNER AND WELFORD.

THE

WORK OF THE HOLY SPIRIT.

BY

JAMES S. CANDLISH, D.D.,
PROFESSOR OF SYSTEMATIC THEOLOGY IN THE FREE CHURCH COLLEGE, GLASGOW

CONTENTS.

PART I.

THE HOLY SPIRIT.

		PAGE
Chapter I.	The Spirit of God in the Old Testament,	11
,, II.	The Spirit of God in the New Testament,	21
,, III.	The Spirit of God in the Creeds of the Church,	29

PART II.

THE WORK OF THE HOLY SPIRIT.

		PAGE
Chapter I.	The Work of the Holy Spirit on Christ,	37
,, II.	The Sending of the Holy Spirit by Christ,	43
,, III.	The Work of the Spirit in the External Call of the Word,	49
,, IV.	The Work of the Spirit in Conviction,	58
,, V.	The Work of the Spirit in Conversion,	67
,, VI.	The Work of the Spirit uniting us to Christ,	85
,, VII.	The Work of the Spirit in Sanctification,	89
,, VIII.	The Work of the Spirit as a Witness and Teacher,	97
,, IX.	The Work of the Spirit as our Helper in Prayer,	106
,, X.	The Comforting Work of the Holy Spirit,	111

INTRODUCTORY.

THE work of the Holy Spirit of God in our salvation from sin is known to us only through the Christian revelation recorded in Scripture. The blessed and beneficent effects of it are indeed to be traced in the great improvement and elevation of the moral state of mankind under the influence of Christianity, and these afford evidence of a strictly historical nature that Christianity is indeed of divine origin. But we could not from these effects alone ascertain with any degree of minuteness the nature and working of the divine agency by which they are produced. Such information, however, is given us in the inspired records, especially of the New Testament, from which we learn what Jesus and His apostles taught as to the way in which the hearts and lives of men are renewed and purified, as well as how they are reconciled to God. Our inquiry therefore into this subject is to be prosecuted in the first place and chiefly by the study of the Bible, although we may expect to find the conclusions to which that leads us confirmed by the experience through which we pass if we obey the practical precepts and directions of the gospel.

The salvation that Christianity brings to sinners is represented in Scripture as consisting of two principal parts—deliverance from guilt, condemnation, and wrath, which is ascribed directly to the work of the Lord Jesus Christ for us; and deliverance from the love and habit and power of sin in ourselves, which is represented as especially the work of the Paraclete, the Holy Spirit, whom Jesus said His Father would send in His name. It is the latter of these that is the subject of this treatise; and in order to ascertain in a methodical way the teaching of Scripture on it, it will be suitable to consider it under two general heads—the Holy Spirit Himself, and the work that He does in our salvation. These accordingly will be the two principal parts of this handbook.

PART I.

THE HOLY SPIRIT.

CHAPTER I.

THE SPIRIT OF GOD IN THE OLD TESTAMENT.

THE name "spirit of God" is one that occurs very often in the Bible from its first page to its last, and in many different connections, so that it is not always easy to determine what is meant by it. The words in the original languages rendered "spirit" in English mean primarily "wind" or "breath;" and like similar words in most languages, are used in a figurative sense to denote the soul or mind of man. The breath that is in his nostrils, that never ceases to respire as long as there is life in the body, and that forms in articulate sounds the expression of his thoughts and feelings, is taken to represent the life itself or the thinking self-conscious "I," that he feels himself to be. In like manner, the phrase "spirit of God" is sometimes used for the life that is in God, or God himself as a spiritual being. In Ps. cxxxix. 7, "Whither shall I go from thy spirit?" is parallel to "Whither shall I flee from thy presence?" and the next verse, "If I ascend up into heaven, thou art there," shows that God's spirit here means the same as God Himself. In Isa. xl. 13, "the spirit of the LORD" is also parallel to "him," and is rendered by Paul (1 Cor. ii. 16) "the mind of the Lord." It has the same meaning in

Zech. vi. 8; and the similar word "soul" is used of God in Isa. xlii. 1, Matt. xii. 18.

But much more frequently the phrase Spirit of God is used after a more literal analogy, and denotes a power or influence coming forth from God, as the breath comes out of the mouth of man. As the thunder is called in Biblical poetry the voice of the Lord (Ps. xviii. 13, xxix. 3-9), so the stormy wind is sometimes called the breath of God, "the blast of the breath of his nostrils" (Ex. xv. 8; Ps. xviii. 15; Job iv. 9; Isa. xxx. 33; and in the New Testament, 2 Thess. ii. 8); and the notion of the breath of God is also connected with the milder and beneficent agencies of the wind in nature, as in Ps. civ. 30, where the renewal of the face of the earth, and the reproduction of living things, are ascribed to the spirit or breath of God. So in the narrative of the Creation, at the very outset it is said, "the spirit of God moved on the face of the waters" (Gen. i. 2). This may be taken in close connection with what follows : "And God said, Let there be light : and there was light" (v. 3); the spirit being, as it were, the breath of God that forms His word of creative power. So it seems to be meant in Ps. xxxiii. 6, "By the word of the Lord were the heavens made ; and all the host of them by the breath of his mouth." Again, in Job xxvi. 13, it is said in reference to creation, "By his spirit the heavens are furnished;" where it is not so much the idea of breath, as that of wisdom, that seems to be meant.

More particularly the breath of life in man is said to have been breathed into his nostrils by God (Gen. ii. 7); and this is especially applied to the intellectual life of man, Job xxxii. 8, "there is a spirit in man, and the breath of the Almighty giveth them understanding;" xxxiii. 4, "The spirit of God hath made me, and the breath of the Almighty giveth me life." So it is said, by a somewhat different figure, "the spirit of man is the lamp of the LORD, searching all the innermost parts of the belly" (Prov. xx. 27), where reference seems to be made to what we call the voice of conscience. Compare Rom. ii. 14, 15. The same thing may also be meant in Gen. vi. 3 : "The LORD said, My spirit shall not strive with (or rule in) man for ever, for that he also is flesh : yet shall his days be an hundred and twenty years." The only previous reference to the spirit of God in man was in Gen. ii. 7, where it is described as the source of his life. The meaning, however, cannot be that individual men should not live for ever ; for that had been made abundantly plain before : it must refer to the race as a whole, and declare that after a respite of 120 years it should be swept away; as it was by the flood. If the rendering "strive" be correct, the passage would imply that man's God-given soul is a moral witness against sin, as we see in the narratives of the remorse of Adam and Cain (Gen. iii. 7-10, iv. 14, 15) : if the translation should be "rule, or abide, in man," then it would simply denote the presence and power of that spirit of life that God breathed into man at the first. However this may be, it seems clear that the godly Israelites recognised the voice of God in the teachings of their own consciences. Of this we have a striking illustration in Ps. xvi. 7 :—

> "I will bless the LORD, who hath given me counsel;
> Yea, my reins instruct me in the night seasons."

The same thing is described in the two parallel clauses, first from the side of God and then from that of man. It is the Lord's counsel that has moved the Psalmist to choose Him as his portion ; but it has come to him by the voice of his own reins or heart. In like manner, an evil conscience was regarded as of God, and the evil spirit that troubled Saul after his sin and rejection by God is called "an evil spirit from the LORD" (1 Sam. xvi. 14), "an evil spirit of God, of the LORD" (1 Sam. xviii. 10, xix. 9); and even absolutely "a spirit of God" (1 Sam. xvi. 23). These phrases can hardly mean a wicked spirit possessing the unfaithful king, like the demoniacs of whom we read in the New Testament : they rather denote his own guilty conscience stirred up by divine influence to accuse and torment him.

But besides these general uses of the name spirit or breath of

God, for the working of His power and wisdom in the world of nature and in the soul of man, we find it employed in a peculiarly distinctive sense in the region of God's special covenant relations with Israel as His people. There it appears as a gift bestowed upon selected persons, giving them power and capacity for various functions in the service of God and of His people. It is said of Abraham, that he was a prophet (Gen. xx. 7), which according to the explanations given later would imply the possession of the spirit of God, though in the narrative in Genesis it was only said before that the word of the Lord came to Abraham (Gen. xvi. 1), and that the Lord appeared to him (Gen. xvii. 1, xviii. 1). Pharaoh is represented as calling Joseph "a man in whom the spirit of God is," forasmuch as God had showed him what was to come, and he was discreet and wise (Gen. xli. 38, 39). Then Moses is described as having the spirit of God upon him, though this is said only incidentally (Num. xi. 17, 25), and no express account is given of the bestowal of the spirit upon him, except that when he was called to be the deliverer of Israel God said, " I will be with thy mouth and teach thee what thou shalt speak" (Ex. iv. 12); and it is implied through all the narrative of his work that he was taught and guided by God. Bezaleel, the chief artificer of the tabernacle in the wilderness, is said to have been filled with the spirit of God in all wisdom for his work (Ex. xxxi. 3); and when the work of Moses in governing the people was to be shared with seventy of the elders, we read that God took of the spirit that was upon him, and gave it unto them (Num. xi. 17, 25). From the context of these passages we may see, that while the spirit of God is spoken of in them, not as being in all men, as in the texts formerly adduced, but as a special gift to particular persons; still this gift is closely connected, on the one hand with what we should call natural endowments, and on the other hand with the presence of God Himself. The spirit, in these cases, is something more specific and individual than the rational soul or conscience common to all men, but it is not entirely separate from that, but simply high and special powers of intellect or moral sense, wisdom, unselfishness, godliness. These qualities, too, are not merely regarded as gifts of God in general, but the insight, guidance, and power that they give, are viewed as really the teaching and help of God Himself. As man's intellectual nature in general is represented as due to God's having breathed into him the breath of life; so special powers of mind or soul are considered to be due to a special communion with God on the part of those who have them.

In the days of the Judges, the spirit of the LORD is spoken of in connection with deeds of courage and prowess, and even of physical strength, as it is said to have come on Othniel (Judg. iii. 10), Gideon (vi. 34), Jephthah (xi. 29), and Samson (xiii. 25, xiv. 6, 19, xv. 14). In these cases there is no direct reference to moral qualities; but it is to be observed that they were all men who believed in Jehovah, and were fighting for His cause and His people. In many cases the special token and proof of the presence and working of the spirit of God was prophecy; and so in Hos. ix. 7, "the prophet" is used as a parallel to "the man that hath the spirit;" and in Joel ii. 28, when God promises to pour out His spirit on all flesh, the effect is to be, "your sons and your daughters shall prophesy," etc. But it would seem that in early times the notion of prophecy in Israel was similar to that entertained in other ancient nations, unpremeditated utterance of lofty, vehement, or mysterious language, often in a state of trance or ecstasy approaching that of madness. As in such utterances the deliberative judgment is not in exercise, they seemed more directly due to a divine impulse, and so were ascribed to the Spirit of God, whatever was their moral character and tendency, and without being regarded as conveying a message from God that ought to be observed and obeyed. It is only by some such idea as this that we can understand how Joshua could propose to forbid Eldad and Medad prophesying in the camp (Num. xi. 28). So, too, Saul is represented as prophesying, when under the power of the evil spirit of God, he tried to smite David with his javelin (1 Sam. xviii. 10, 11), as well as when the spirit of God that was on the prophets came upon him (1 Sam. xix. 23. 24). This is probably the explanation of the strange pictorial vision of Micaiah (1 Kings xxii. 19-23), in which the spirit of prophecy is personified. The lying spirit is not an evil spirit in the New Testament sense; neither can it be absolutely identified with the Divine Spirit; it is rather a personification of the prophetic *afflatus*, the impulse to rapt enthusiastic utterance, considered as a gift of God, in itself neither morally good nor evil, but becoming evil in the mouths of evil men bent on flattering the king. The breath of the Almighty gave them the power of fervent impassioned language, and thus enabled them to persuade Ahab to his destruction. Such seems to be, expressed in modern language, the substantial meaning of that remarkable vision: and it rests on the general conception of the spirit of God as the author of all mental powers and manifestations, and more especially of those in which human deliberation falls into the background. The constraining power of the spiritual impulse to prophecy appears in the case of Elihu (Job xxxii. 18-20), and Jeremiah (xx. 9), as also in Ps. xlv. 1. As God's training of His people advanced from stage to stage, He taught them, that the true test of prophecy as His word to them is not the enthusiastic and unusual mode of its utterance, but its moral power over the hearts and lives of the hearers (Jer. xxiii. 22-29); and its fulfilment in the course of Providence (Deut. xvii. 21, 22). When this came to be known, there are no longer such ascriptions of evil powers and influences to the spirit of God as in earlier days.[1] The divine agency continues indeed to be recognised in the downward career that sinners are ever prone to run: but this is expressed in the way of God leaving them to themselves and to the natural consequences of their own

---

[1] The latest instance that approaches this is in Acts xxi. 4, where the advice not to go up to Jerusalem is said to have been given to Paul "through the Spirit," but disregarded by him, unquestionably in accordance with the will of God.

sin (Ps. lxxviii. 29-31, lxxxi. 12; Ezek. xx. 25, 26; Hos. iv. 17; and most distinctly Rom. i. 24-32).

In the later portions of the Old Testament we also find the spirit of God more and more associated with moral qualities. The epithet holy is given to the spirit of God in Ps. li. 11, where the psalmist is penetrated with a penitent sense of sin, and in Isa. lxiii. 10, 11, where reference is made to the history of the Exodus and wilderness journey. When the prophet says, "they grieved his holy spirit," that phrase may simply refer to God Himself as the Holy One; but when he says, "He put his holy spirit in the midst of them," it must mean the spirit given to Moses and the elders, here more especially described as holy. Similarly in Neh. ix. 20, in reference to the same history, it is said, "Thou gavest also thy good spirit to instruct them;" and from the context it is plain that moral goodness must be meant: and in another of the penitential psalms (cxliii. 10), God's spirit is also called good in the same sense. It is clear, therefore, that latterly at least the spirit of God was recognised as the source not only of power, and wisdom, and prophecy, but of moral goodness as well; and that this aspect of it becomes gradually the most prominent. There are many places in which the spirit of God, though not expressly called holy, is described as giving the fear of the Lord (Isa. xi. 2-5), judgment and righteousness (Isa. xxxii. 15-17), devotion to the Lord (Isa. xliv. 3-5), hearty obedience (Ezek. xxxvi. 26, 27), penitence and prayer (Zech. xii. 10). But the general bestowal of the spirit as the source of holiness is spoken of as a thing of the future, one of the blessings of the promised reign of God over His people. In the theocracy in Israel, the spirit of God had been given to certain chosen men as leaders and rulers of the nation, and doubtless wherever there was genuine godliness, that was due to the working of the spirit; but there is no indication that the mass of the nation, though the professed people of God, was filled with the spirit, in the sense in which the Christian Church after the Pentecostal gift was so. What distinguished the chosen people as a nation from others, was the possession of the revelation and law of God. "He showeth his word unto Jacob, his statutes and his judgments unto Israel. He hath not dealt so with any nation, and as for his judgments, they have not known them" (Ps. cxlvii. 19, 20). This was done through Moses and the prophets: but the higher blessing of being all directly taught of God, having His law written in their hearts, and His spirit poured out upon them all, was longed for by Moses (Num. xi. 29), and foretold by the prophets as one of the good things of the latter days, to be bestowed in connection with the Messianic salvation (Isa. liv. 13; Jer. xxxi. 33, 34; Joel ii. 28, 29). It came to be perceived more and more in the course of Israel's history, that the want of this was the great obstacle to the reformation and restoration of the nation as the people of God. The prophets gave solemn and awful warnings, which generally made an impression at the time, and when aided by the kings and civil authorities, produced an outward reformation in the order and conduct of the state: but new forms of evil were ever coming up, as old ones were banished: formalism and hypocrisy took the place of idolatry and debauchery; and the prophets after the exile, though they had not to denounce the same sins that their predecessors rebuked, still must address the people as ungodly and backsliding, and look forward to some more effective cure for their corruption in the time to come. Such a cure was to be found only in the outpouring of the spirit of God on the people, to change their hearts and turn them to the Lord. Jeremiah foretells that there is to be a new covenant, in which the law shall be written in the people's hearts, and they shall not be dependent on the teaching of others, but all shall know the Lord (Jer. xxxi. 31-34). Ezekiel speaks of the same blessing, and connects it expressly with the spirit of God (Ezek. xxxvi. 25-27). In Isaiah, and especially in the later prophecies in that book, we find these promises connected with the coming of the Son of David, the Lord's servant, who is anointed with His spirit (Isa. xi., xii., lx., lxi.); and in Zechariah and Malachi there are similar representations.

It was in the line and in the spirit of these prophecies, that after a long term of silence in the divine oracles, John the son of the priest Zacharias came from the wilderness where he had dwelt alone with God, calling Israel to repentance, and baptizing in Jordan those who complied with his call. What he demanded was not mere sorrow for past sin, or outward reformation of conduct, but a change of mind, for that is the real meaning of the word rendered "repentance" in English. It is the same change that is spoken of in the Old Testament as circumcising the heart (Jer. iv. 4), making a new heart and a new spirit (Ezek. xviii. 35). John called for this from all, even from the Pharisees and the Sadducees, the most religious and influential of the people; and he symbolized their cleansing from sin, by plunging them in the water of Jordan to rise out of it again as it were new men. This was to be the preparation for the kingdom or reign of God, which the old prophets had foretold as future, and which he now announced as at hand. At the same time he declared that he was not the Messiah, that he only baptized with water, but that One greater than he was coming after him, who should baptize with the Holy Spirit, that is to say, who should fulfil these old prophecies, and really give the spirit of God as a renewing and sanctifying influence to the mass of men.

In all these Old Testament representations, it is to be observed, the spirit of God is regarded not merely as a gift bestowed by God yet separate from Himself, but, according to the original meaning of the phrase, as the very breath of God, so that it is God Himself who is with men and teaches them inwardly, when His Spirit is bestowed on them. The same things are said to be done sometimes by God and sometimes by the spirit of God. For God to write His law in the heart of His people (Jer. xxxi. 33), is the same as to put His spirit within them (Ezek. xxvi. 27); and in another place it is said, "The LORD of hosts shall be . . . for a spirit of judgment to him that sitteth in judgment" (Isa. xxviii. 5, 6). So also in the last words of David we read, "The spirit of the LORD spake by me, and his word was upon my tongue. The God of Israel said, The Rock of Israel spake to me" (2 Sam. xxiii. 2, 3). Thus the idea of the spirit of God is somewhat like that of the word of God, or the angel (*i.e.* messenger or message) of the Lord, both sent from God and yet Himself God. These peculiar representations led many of the Jewish teachers to recognise a certain distinction in the Divine Being, between God as He is in Himself, as the infinite, invisible, incomprehensible First Cause, and God as He made Himself known to men by that Wisdom and Power, that are truly divine, yet seen in the works of Creation, Providence, and Grace. More than this general idea of distinction in the Godhead, and of a spirit working in men that is both of God and also God Himself, cannot be said to have been revealed in Old Testament times, when the great fact of God reconciling the world to Himself was only dimly seen in the future: the distinction was apt to be refined away into a philosophical abstraction, and its full meaning as a religious truth was not yet seen. More particularly from the Old Testament alone the difference between the word and the spirit of God could not be clearly gathered; and there was a tendency to identify them and recognise only a twofold distinction in the Godhead. That which distinctly revealed the Trinity in the Godhead, which the older oracles but hinted at, and philosophy uncertainly groped after, was the manifestation of Jesus Christ as the Word made flesh, and His teaching about Himself as truly God, and about the Spirit of God that He not only received, but promised to give.

CHAPTER II.

THE SPIRIT OF GOD IN THE NEW TESTAMENT.

WHAT our Lord Himself taught about the Spirit of God is quite in harmony with the Old Testament promises, and the proclamation of His forerunner the Baptist; while it throws new light on what the earlier revelation still left dark. His more popular teaching, which was mostly given in Galilee, has been reported chiefly by the first three Evangelists. We learn from these, that he spoke of the Spirit of God being upon Him, as when in the synagogue at Nazareth he applied to himself the words of the Servant of Jehovah in Isa. lxi., "The Spirit of the Lord is upon me, because he anointed me to preach good tidings to the poor," etc. (Luke iv. 18–20); and the truth of this claim was shown by the graciousness and power of his words causing astonishment to those who heard them,—an effect which is described also by Matthew (xiii. 54) and Mark (vi. 2). More particularly, Jesus declared that it was by the Spirit of God that He cast out demons, and that this proved that the reign of God was come upon them, *i.e.* that God was really setting up His kingdom on earth (Matt. xii. 28). In Luke's account, the expression is "by the finger of God" (xi. 20), which might merely denote divine power, but that Jesus meant to indicate the moral character of His power as holy, is clear from the obvious gist of His argument against those who ascribed His expulsion of demons to Beelzebub. Since the kingdom of God is, according to all the Old Testament representations, a kingdom of holiness, the Spirit by which it is established must be holy; and by its opposition to all unclean spirits is recognised as the Spirit of God. Hence the guilt of speaking against or reviling the Holy Spirit is immeasurably greater than that of speaking against the Son of man. The Messiah may be reviled ignorantly, by men who do not see His divine Sonship in the human nature which He wears; and for such sin there is forgiveness by God's grace to those who repent: but if a man reviles that very spirit of holiness whereby God reveals himself, he sets himself against holiness itself, seen and known as such; and how shall such an one be delivered from sin and obtain forgiveness? Jesus thus distinguishes the Spirit of God from Himself the Son of man; while He speaks of both as the objects of blasphemy, *i.e.* reviling, an offence that can properly be committed only against a person, not against a mere power or influence.

It is also taught in the discourses of Jesus recorded in the Synoptic Gospels, that the Spirit of God, the Holy Spirit, that was on Him, was to speak in His disciples, and this seems to have been said by Him on more than one occasion. Matthew reports it in connection with the sending out of the twelve (x. 20); Luke gives it along with the warning against blaspheming the Holy Spirit in a somewhat loosely-connected series of discourses at a later time (xii. 12); and Mark embodies it in our Lord's discourse to His disciples about the future on the Mount of Olives (xiii. 11), in a connection in which Luke reports him as saying, " I will give you a mouth and wisdom " (xxi. 15). This is one of the indications in these Gospels, that Jesus gives the Spirit, or as the Baptist put it, baptizes with the Holy Spirit. He declares that the Father will give the Holy Spirit to them that ask him (Luke xi. 13); and Luke also records sayings of Jesus after His resurrection, that clearly point to the gift of the Spirit as bestowed by Him on His disciples according to the promise of the Father (Luke xxiv. 49; Acts i. 8).

This is more fully declared in the great farewell discourse after the last Supper, recorded by John (xiv.-xvi.), in which Jesus speaks of the Holy Spirit as to be sent by the Father at His request, to supply to the disciples His own absence. There He not only uses the personal pronouns in reference to the Spirit (see especially xiv. 26 and xv. 26), but promises that the Spirit will be to them what He had been in His earthly life, "another Comforter." The word in the original is Paraclete, and is only used elsewhere, as applied to Christ, by John in his First Epistle (ii. 1), where it is rendered Advocate in English. This is its literal meaning, one who is called in, to give instruction, encouragement, or help, or to appear and plead on our behalf before an adversary or a judge. All this Jesus had done for His disciples during His earthly ministry. He had taught them the secrets of the kingdom of God ; He had been ever at hand when called for to give help in danger, as in the storm on the sea of Galilee, or to solve difficulties, as when they brought questions that perplexed them to Him to answer ; He had spoken in their defence when they were accused by the Pharisees of breaking the Sabbath and neglecting the traditions of the scribes ; He had prayed for them to God when they were exposed to the temptations of the world and its prince. But now that His bodily presence was to be no longer with them, He promises to send another advocate to do for them what He had hitherto done in person. They felt not only the want of His powerful help in view of the difficulties that stared them in the face as they were to carry on the work He had begun, but more especially the loss of His affectionate loving fellowship : and this feeling, which chiefly filled their hearts, could not be met by the promise of a mere impersonal divine influence that would give them wisdom and courage. To speak, in such an hour, of a mere power or influence from God in figurative language that would naturally suggest a person, would be a cruel mockery of their sorrow, which we cannot ascribe to Jesus. He must have meant His words to be understood, in their obvious literal meaning, of a divine Agent as truly personal as Himself.

The presence of the Holy Spirit was to be, in a true and higher sense, Jesus' own presence. He speaks of His coming to them, and of the Spirit's coming, as if these expressions both referred to the same thing (John xiv. 16, 18, xvi. 13, 16). He was to be with them by the Spirit. Hitherto He had been with them in the flesh; they had known Him, just as men know their fellow-men, through the body He had assumed; they had seen its form and heard His voice with their bodily senses. This was no longer to be; but He was to manifest Himself to them in a higher and better way than that, by the Spirit, who should take of His and show it to them, so that He should really be with them again, by His Spirit having fellowship with their spirits. His coming thus to them would also be the coming of the Father (John xiv. 23, 24), as when they really knew Him they should know the Father also.

It is remarkable, that the evangelist who has recorded those sayings of Jesus does not in his own writings speak of the Spirit in such a way as clearly to imply personality; but uses figures, such as the anointing (1 John ii. 20, 27), and God giving us of His Spirit (1 John iv. 13), which seem to refer to a power or influence. This may prove that John did not so fully unfold the revelation given by Jesus as we might have expected: but it shows us all the more how true and faithful is his record of Jesus' words.

In the Epistles of James, Peter, and Jude, there is a similar indistinctness of teaching. The brevity and practical character of these letters sufficiently account for little being said of the Holy Spirit; and while there is nothing that certainly implies His personality, there is nothing in the slightest degree inconsistent with it. In the Book of Acts and in the Apocalypse the Spirit is described as speaking and using personal pronouns of Himself (Acts viii. 29, x. 19, 20, xi. 12, xiii. 2; Rev. ii. 7, xiv. 13, xxii. 17).

In the Epistle to the Hebrews, whose great theme is the contrast of the Jewish and Christian dispensations, the Holy Spirit comes into view as given in the former to prophets and other inspired men, and in the latter to all the people of God, but chiefly as manifested in miraculous gifts.

But the fullest teaching about the Spirit in the New Testament is to be found in the Epistles of Paul, which most distinctly unfold the nature of Christianity, especially in its inward and experimental aspects. In these Epistles there are attributed to the Holy Spirit various things that can belong only to a personal being, such as "mind," in the sense of purpose or intention as expressed in intercession (Rom. viii. 27), "searching all things" (1 Cor. ii. 11), "dividing to every man severally as he will" (1 Cor. xii. 11), "being grieved" (Eph. iv. 30). Paul calls the Spirit, the Spirit of Christ (Rom. viii. 9), the Spirit of God's Son (Gal. iv. 4); speaks of Christ being in us, and Christ's Spirit being in us as the same thing (Rom. viii. 9, 10); and ascribes the same work indifferently now to God, now to Christ, and now to the Holy Spirit.

In the teaching of Paul the Holy Spirit is represented as dwelling in Christians as the principle of moral and religious life. This is found in all his Epistles, from the earliest (1 Thess. i. 6, iv. 8; 2 Thess. ii. 13), through the central group (Rom. viii. 2–17; Gal. v. 13–26; 1 Cor. ii. 12–16) on to the latest (Eph. iii. 16; 2 Tim. i. 7, 14), while in them all the Spirit is also recognised as the source of supernatural gifts, such as prophecy, tongues, miracles. But it is hardly correct to say, as some have done, that the former of these representations is peculiar to Paul, and that the other New Testament writers only speak of the Spirit as the source of miraculous gifts. The notion of the Spirit of God as the giver, not only of prophetic or miraculous gifts, but of holiness, is found even in the Old Testament (Ezek. xxxvi. 27; Ps. cxliii. 10); and is implied in the words of John the Baptist, that the Messiah should baptize with the Holy Spirit. It could hardly be absent from the mind of any devout Israelite, and seems to be involved in the very name, the Holy Spirit, which is not found in the earlier Old Testament writings, but which is used by all the penmen of the New Testament. There are also express recognitions of this function of the Spirit of God in 1 Pet. i. 2, iv. 14; Jude 19, 20; 1 John iii. 11, and iv. 16; and perhaps in Jas. iv. 5, as well as in our Lord's conversation with Nicodemus (John iii. 3–8). These passages show at least that the idea was not unknown, though it is undoubtedly true, that Paul has unfolded it much more fully than the other New Testament writers; and that in the Epistle to the Hebrews views of the Christian life are given which do not require the consideration of this function of the Holy Spirit.

It has also been thought by some, that Paul's conception of the Holy Spirit, as the principle of the Christian life, does not require a recognition of anything more than a power proceeding from God; and that the passages where Paul ascribes knowledge, purpose, and will to the Spirit, are merely personifications. But it seems clear that what Paul meant to teach was not merely that a power from God is at work in believers, but that God Himself works in them. The Spirit of God is not indeed in his view an independent personality; that is not implied in the doctrine of the personality of the Spirit; but as the spirit of a man is to the man, so according to Paul the Spirit of God is to God, in one sense the same, but in another sense distinct. The principle of the Christian life is not a mere impersonal power, but God Himself in a mysterious way dwelling and working in the soul. But it is God working in man to lead him to God as He is above him; hence the Spirit of God that works in him must be distinguished from God, yet not as a different being, but just as the spirit or mind of a man may be distinguished from the man, and may be said to know the things of a man (1 Cor. ii. 10-16).

Paul's doctrine of the Spirit in this place is parallel to John's doctrine of the Word (John i. 1-18); and both point to an analogy between the nature of man and that of God. In man we must distinguish the soul itself from its functions of understanding, feeling, and will, which are yet one with it; and in the divine Being, revelation teaches us to distinguish the Father, His Son or Word, and His Spirit, who are yet one God. The doctrine of the Spirit of God as a divine person rests on the more clearly revealed doctrine of the Word or Son of God who became incarnate in Jesus Christ. If we are satisfied that the Word is the same as the Son of God, and is not merely a divine power or influence moving and strengthening the man Christ Jesus, nor yet a created and finite being, but one possessing all the attributes and receiving the worship proper to God; then we must conceive the Deity as not absolutely simple in all respects, but having a certain mysterious distinction in the manner of subsistence, on the one hand as Father, and on the other hand as Son; the Father being God as He is the source of all being, and the Son, or Word, God as He knows and manifests Himself. But if any such distinction is recognised in the Deity, then the way in which Jesus and His apostles speak of the Holy Spirit requires us to regard the Being so described as similar in nature to the Word; and so to recognise, not merely a twofold, but a threefold distinction in God. The doctrine of the Holy Spirit depends upon that of the person of Christ, and comes after it, both historically and logically. Jesus taught His disciples to believe in Him as the Son of God, before He spoke to them of the Holy Spirit, as another Advocate; and while the Church implicitly believed in both from the first, it was not till after she had, by much discussion, come to a distinct understanding of her faith in Christ as divine, that she arrived at similar clearness in regard to the Holy Spirit. When, too, the doctrine of the Spirit came to be discussed, appeal was made to the previously ascertained doctrine of the true deity of Christ. If it were possible to believe that Jesus was a mere man, then there would be no antecedent reason to recognise any distinction in the deity beyond that of attributes or powers, such as the Platonists and Alexandrian Jews held; and what is said about the Spirit might be regarded as mere figurative or exaggerated descriptions of a divine influence. But if, as we believe to be the fact, we cannot do justice to the character and claims of Jesus or to the worship paid Him by His disciples, without acknowledging Him to be truly God; then we see from His relation to the Father, that the sayings which speak personally of the Spirit may be taken more literally, while at the same time, if they are the teaching not merely of a man sent from God, but of one who is Himself God, they cannot be so freely handled as on the other theory they must be.

Were we to confine our view of the New Testament doctrine on this subject to passages that speak especially of the Holy Spirit; we might be apt to think, that those which distinctly suggest a personal being are but few, and balanced by others which point rather to an impersonal power; and that where exegetical considerations are so doubtful, the preference is due to the view which implies no transcendently mysterious doctrine, and only requires allowance to be made for some rather bold personifications. But the matter will appear differently, if we consider, that the understanding of what is meant by the Holy Spirit in the New Testament depends on the answer to the larger question, What is the Christian idea of God? If that implies, that the divine Being is not an absolutely simple unity, but is distinguished in itself as Father and Son; if Christians are consecrated in baptism to the name of the Father and of the Son and of the Holy Spirit (Matt. xxviii. 19); if in the bestowal of spiritual gifts on the Church there are recognised one Spirit, one Lord, one God and Father of all (1 Cor. xii. 4–6; Eph. iv. 4–6); and if blessings are invoked from the Lord Jesus Christ and the Holy Spirit as well as from God (2 Cor. xiii. 14); the evidence that the New Testament represents the Spirit as a person, in the same sense as the Word, is seen to be much more extensive and conclusive.

CHAPTER III.

THE SPIRIT OF GOD IN THE CREEDS OF THE CHURCH.

THE truth implied in the various representations of Scripture about the Spirit has generally been expressed by theologians in the statement, that the Spirit of God is not merely a power or influence from God, but God Himself as working in the minds and hearts of men, or in other words, a divine person, though not separate or separable from the Father and the Son, but one with them in being, in perfections, and in acting. When we assert the personality of the Holy Spirit, we use the word person, not in the sense it has when applied to men, but in a modified and quite special sense. We employ it to denote a mysterious distinction in the divine Being, that Scripture makes known to us, the nature of which we cannot positively conceive; but in virtue of which we believe that the Father, Son, and Holy Spirit are truly distinct, and each is truly God; while yet there are not three Gods, but one God only. We do not profess to be able to explain wherein the distinction lies; we can only say negatively, that it is more than a distinction of different modes of viewing the same being, as when we think of God as almighty, wise, and good; but less than that of different beings, as when we distinguish God, angels, and men. The word person is really only a distant and imperfect analogy,—a term thrown out at an object which we cannot grasp in thought. It has a certain justification from the fact that Scripture uses personal pronouns, *I, Thou, He,* of the Father, the Son, and the Holy

Spirit, and represents them as using these of and to one another; but our use of it does not mean that there are three persons in the same sense in which we speak of three men as three human persons. Indeed it is only in modern times that this meaning of the word person has become common: at the time when it was first applied to the Godhead, it was quite correct to say, that one man might unite in himself three persons, that is, parts or characters; and the difficulty then felt about the word was, that it seemed to make the distinctions in the Godhead too slight; though in modern times, if understood in its ordinary sense, it makes them too great. The fact is, that it was adopted to denote something intermediate between the ancient and the modern meaning. Though we cannot positively explain what that is, it cannot be proved to involve a contradiction that there should be such a distinction in the incomprehensible being of God. This distinction is most clearly revealed to us in Jesus Christ. He spoke of Himself as the Son of God in a peculiar sense, so as to make Himself equal with God (John v. 17-23); as one with the Father (John x. 30-39); as the only one who knows the Father and is known by Him alone (Matt. xi. 27), as deserving supreme and exclusive love from all (Matt. x. 27; Luke xiv. 26); and by His immediate and inspired disciples He is called God and worshipped (John i. 1, xii. 41, xx. 28; Acts vii. 59; Rom. ix. 5; 1 Cor. i. 2; 2 Cor. xii. 8; 1 Pet. iii. 15; Rev. i. 17, v. 8-14). Yet it is equally clear that He is distinct from the Father since He habitually prayed to Him, spoke of Him as sending, commanding, sustaining Him. What this relation of oneness and yet distinction is in itself, we cannot understand; but that there is such a relation, that the Father and the Son are both God and are distinct from one another, and yet are not two but one only, is proved by facts and testimonies too many and too clear to permit us to doubt it. Now in like manner, the Holy Spirit which is given and sent by the Father and the Son, just as the Son is given and sent by the Father is described as having divine attributes, and doing divine works, and is associated with the Father and the Son in the institution of baptism (Matt. xxviii. 19), and in the benediction (1 Cor. xiii. 14). Therefore the great body of Christians have believed that the Holy Spirit, like the Son of God, is truly God, yet distinct from the Father and the Son ; and have expressed what they conceive God's revelation to teach on this subject, by saying, first in the Apostolic Creed, "I believe in the Holy Ghost," that is, not merely, "I believe that there is a Holy Ghost," as I believe the Holy Catholic Church, but "I trust in the Holy Ghost," as I trust in God the Father Almighty, and in Jesus Christ His only Son our Lord.[1] Afterwards, when the true deity of the Holy Spirit was denied by some, the faith of the Church was asserted in this form: "We believe in the Holy Ghost, the Lord, the Giver of life, who proceedeth from the Father, who with the Father and the Son together is worshipped and glorified, who spake by the prophets."[2] The Church of Scotland in all her branches expresses her adherence to these ancient confessions of faith, by teaching her children to say : " There are three Persons in the Godhead, the Father, the Son, and the Holy Ghost, and these three are one God, the same in substance, equal in power and glory." We call the Father, the Son, and the Holy Ghost, persons, because though they are not so called in the Bible, they are represented as using personal pronouns, *I*, *Thou*, *He*, of themselves and each other, *e.g.* John xv. 26, "When the Comforter is come, whom *I* will send unto

---

[1] The distinction between *believing in* an object of faith and simply *believing* is carefully observed in the Creed ; and the former phrase is used in the first three articles, the latter in all the rest. Following many of the Fathers, the Reformers laid great stress upon this, as showing that the relation of believers to the Church is entirely different from their relation to God and Christ. We believe the Church, as we believe the forgiveness of sins, the resurrection of the body, and the life everlasting ; *i.e.* we regard these blessed privileges as true and real ; but we do not believe in them, *i.e.* trust in them, as we do in God the Father, and Jesus Christ, and the Holy Spirit.

[2] *Creed of the First Council of Constantinople*, A.D. 381, commonly called the *Nicene Creed*.

you from the Father, even the Spirit of truth which proceedeth from the Father, *He* shall bear witness of *me;*" xvii. 6, "And now, O Father, glorify *Thou me* with thine own self with the glory which *I* had with *Thee* before the world was;" Acts xiii. 2, "The Holy Ghost said, Separate *Me* Barnabas and Saul for the work whereunto *I* have called them." We say that they are "in the Godhead," and by that we mean, the being or essence of God; and the word "substance" here means the same as "Godhead." What is the essence of God we cannot comprehend; but the Bible says, when it comes nearest to telling us, "God is Spirit" (John iv. 24), "God is Light" (1 John i. 5), "God is Love" (1 John iv. 8, 16). Now the Comforter, whom Jesus associates with the Father and Himself, is Spirit, unseen, yet living and powerful; He is light, as holy; and He is the Spirit of love. When we say that the Holy Spirit is "the same in substance" with the Father, we mean that He has all divine perfections, and is as truly to be worshipped and trusted as the Father and the Son.

We say that the Holy Spirit proceeds from the Father, as Jesus Himself said (John xvi. 26); and we understand that to mean the same as when He is called, as He so often is, the Spirit of God, or from God, that is, as it were, the breath of God. The Father is said to send the Spirit, but the Spirit is never said to send the Father; hence we infer that the order in which they act is not a mere variable one, but depends on their mode of being, in which the Father is of none, while the Spirit is of the Father, not created or made in time, but eternally proceeding, or breathed out, as it were, from the Father. It is because of this mysterious relation that we can say that the Father works by the Spirit, and that our recognition and honour of the Holy Spirit do not detract from the worship due to the Father, but are a part of it.

Then, as we find that the Holy Spirit is also sent by Christ, and is called the Spirit of God's Son; and that Christ is represented as working by the Spirit, we think it proper to say, that the Holy Spirit proceeds from the Son as well as from the Father. Though that is not said in so many words in Scripture, yet we think these other expressions show, that the thing that is meant by them is as true in relation to the Son as to the Father. On this point there is a difference between the Eastern or Greek Church and the Western or Roman; for the theologians of the East did not recognise the force of the arguments just indicated; and thought it better to keep to the express words of Jesus, and say only, that the Holy Spirit proceeds from the Father; while the Western Church added to the Creed the words, "and from the Son" (*Filioque*). The Protestant Churches have generally thought that the doctrine thus asserted is true; but that it is not so clearly revealed, or so practically important, as to warrant a separation of Churches on account of different views about it.

The doctrine of the Holy Spirit being a divine Person, one with God the Father and Jesus Christ His Son, is one that can not only be proved from Scripture as a revealed truth, but also, to some extent, verified in the religious experience of Christians. Every one who is earnestly seeking to live a life of holiness and communion with God, must feel that he has great difficulty and opposition to contend against. The world, with its business, and cares, and pleasures, tends to draw his mind away from thoughts of God and intercourse with Him who is unseen: the passions, or habits of selfishness, sloth, or pride, make him disinclined to the active disinterested love that is the fulfilling of the moral law: strong and subtle temptations often present themselves to him. He cannot overcome these by any efforts or resolutions of his own will; and the divine law, with all its authority and representations of absolute duty, is unable to raise him above them. He is conscious of an experience similar to that which Paul describes in Rom. vii. 14–25. But when he looks to Christ, and trusts in God's grace and love, is he not conscious of another power in him, lifting him above the influence of the world, the flesh, and the devil, and moving him to love and serve God? It is the power of divine grace or love that has taken possession of his soul. There is something in the Christian's experience beyond his own conscious efforts of will or purpose, something that influences him, he cannot tell how or why; it does not come at his will, but often seizes hold of him when he has not been wishing or expecting it; a passage of Scripture, or a truth of religion, or an example of Christian character, may be at one time the means of arousing deep feeling and heavenly aspiration, when at other times these very things may be presented to him without making any impression. This influence that is at work upon him is therefore independent of outward circumstances, as well as of his own will: it is a power not himself that is working for righteousness. But if so, can it be different from that power which so works in the world, and which we believe to be not a mere impersonal stream of tendency, nor a power absolutely inscrutable, of which we can know nothing, but the living God? There is the same reason to believe that the power making for righteousness of which we are conscious in ourselves is personal, as that the power we see in the moral government of the world is so. Yet this power working in us prompts us to adoration, love, and prayer to God as our Father, and to trust in Christ as our Saviour; hence we are naturally led to conclude, that this power, which the Bible calls the Spirit of God, is a divine Person distinct from God the Father and Jesus Christ His Son, though one in character and being with both. So it has been found in the history of the Church that many men, like Thomas Scott [1] and Robert Hall,[2] have been led by their spiritual experience to the Trinitarian doctrine of the Holy Spirit; and generally those who have accepted this doctrine have done so not only because it has appeared to be taught by revelation, but also because it satisfied some of the deepest wants of their consciences and hearts.[3]

[1] See Scott's *Force of Truth*, Part ii.
[2] See Dr. Gregory's *Memoir of Robert Hall*, in *Hall's Works*, vol. vi. p. 52.
[3] See Wace, *Christianity and Morality*, Boyle Lectures, 1875; Lecture vii., "The Doctrine of the Trinity a Moral Revelation."

PART II.

THE WORK OF THE HOLY SPIRIT.

INTRODUCTORY.

IN the Old Testament, as we have already seen, the Spirit of God is described as working in the creation, preservation, and government of the material world. To this agency there is no direct reference in the New Testament, though it is logically presupposed in the fact that various physical as well as moral effects are ascribed to the Spirit of God, such as miracles, speaking with tongues, and the transportation of persons from one place to another (Acts viii. 39, 40). An agent that can produce such effects in the material world, cannot be limited to mental and moral influence; and since the Spirit is called the finger of God (Matt. xii. 28; Luke xi. 20), and identified with God Himself, we cannot doubt that Jesus and His apostles assumed the Old Testament view of God creating and preserving all things by His Spirit as well as by His word, though they had no occasion directly to assert it. As they have not done so, it is well not to enter into speculations on this work of the Spirit further than to observe, that as the doctrine, that God made and sustains all things by His Word, implies that the universe is not only a work of God but a manifestation of Him, so the corresponding doctrine, that God made and sustains all things by His Spirit, shows that God is to be regarded, not merely as a remote First Cause, but as a present agent in all things, in whom we live and move and have our being. And both doctrines together show, that Christianity, which is our fellowship with the Son and the Spirit of God, is a world-wide and world-subduing religion, because it is the communion with those divine agencies by which the whole universe is created, preserved, and governed. This principle underlies the argument of the Epistle to the Hebrews, and Paul's triumphant confidence in Rom. viii. and elsewhere.

But the work of the Spirit that is directly described in the New Testament, is that which has to do immediately with our salvation. That work may be designated generally in our Lord's own words as glorifying Him (John xvi. 14), even as Christ's work was to glorify the Father (John xvii. 4). Now just as Christ's work of glorifying the Father included both a subjective work of making Him known to men—" I manifested thy name unto the men whom thou gavest me out of the world . . . the words which thou gavest me, I have given unto them" (John xvii. 6, 8), and an objective work of satisfying God's justice for them—"for their sakes I sanctify myself" (John xvii. 19); so the work of the Holy Spirit glorifying Jesus may be viewed also as falling into two parts; there is an objective part, which is outside of those who are to be saved, and includes all that the Spirit does to make Jesus glorious, and manifest Him as such; and a subjective part which is within the souls of men, and includes what He does to enable us to see Christ to be glorious, and to give glory to Him by faith, love, and obedience. The objective or outward work of the Spirit includes His work on Christ, His being sent by Christ, and His presenting Christ to the world in the Word: the subjective or inward work of the Spirit includes His operations in the soul, convincing, converting, sanctifying, teaching, and comforting.

CHAPTER I.

THE WORK OF THE HOLY SPIRIT ON CHRIST.

THE New Testament is pre-eminently the dispensation of the Spirit, fulfilling the promises that God would pour out His Spirit on all flesh (Joel ii. 28), put His Spirit within His people's hearts, and so write His law there (Ezek. xxxvi. 26, 27). This was also predicted to be done through the Servant of Jehovah, the root out of the stem of Jesse, who was to be Himself anointed with the Spirit of God (Isa. xi. 1-4, xlii. 1-4, lxi. 1-3). Accordingly we find in the New Testament that the Holy Spirit is represented primarily as working upon and in Jesus Christ.

In the first place, the Holy Spirit is described as the agent in the miraculous conception of Jesus (Matt. i. 20; Luke i. 35). Though this fact is mentioned explicitly only by these evangelists, their accounts are manifestly independent, and while varying in details agree in substance. The one may represent the report transmitted from Joseph, and the other that coming from Mary. But if not expressly stated, it is presupposed by other New Testament writers, that the beginning of Jesus' human life was not an ordinary one. John reports His saying, "that which is begotten of the flesh is flesh," and therefore needs to be begotten again: but He excludes Himself when He says, "*ye* must be born again;" hence we may infer that He was in some peculiar way begotten not of the flesh but of the Spirit. Paul says that God sent His own Son in the likeness of sinful flesh, and that while He was born of a woman, of the seed of David according to the flesh, He knew no sin. Since all men born according to the ordinary law of nature inherit sin and death from Adam, He who has no sin and saves His people from their sin must needs have been begotten of the Holy Spirit.

In virtue of this agency it was that He grew up filled with wisdom, and the grace of God was upon Him (Luke ii. 40); that He advanced in wisdom and stature, and in favour with God and men (Luke ii. 52), needing no repentance or conversion, but holy, harmless, undefiled, tempted in all things like as we are, yet without sin (Heb. iv. 15, vii. 26).

The holiness of the human nature of our Lord is not to be ascribed directly to its union to the divine nature by the Incarnation. The proper effect of that was to elevate it to the highest dignity, inasmuch as it became the human nature of the eternal Son of God, the soul and body that was for ever a part of His very self. But this wonderful union did not make His soul or body one whit less truly human; and the holiness he had in His human nature is human holiness, not something above our nature, but the very perfection and crown of it; and in this He is like His brethren, receiving the aid of the Holy Spirit. His being God did not make the preservation of holiness in an ungodly world at all more easy to His flesh and blood, nay His task was all the harder. Hence we read that He received the Holy Spirit, was filled with the Spirit, led of the Spirit, anointed with the Holy Spirit; that He was much in prayer to God, and was encouraged by voices from heaven, and strengthened by an angel.

The various points or stages in His life on earth, at which special mention is made of His being under the influence of the Spirit, are worthy of notice.

The first is when He entered on His public work, identifying Himself with those whom John called to repentance, by receiving baptism from one who confessed that he had need to be baptized by Jesus. Then He saw the heavens opened, and the Holy Spirit descending on Him in visible form as a dove, and heard a voice from heaven saying, "This is my beloved Son, in whom I am well pleased." This was for Him a testimony of His Father's approval, which would strengthen and encourage His human soul; and it would seem that along with it there was not a mere symbol, but an actual communication to His human nature of the gracious influence of the Holy Spirit. Immediately afterwards we read that Jesus was full of the Holy Spirit (Luke iv. 1), and we can hardly avoid connecting that with the occurrence at His baptism. He was now endowed to the full in His humanity with all the wisdom, and power, and zeal, and love, needed for carrying out His great commission as the Saviour of the world.

Then He was led (Matt. iv. 1; Luke iv. 1), or as Mark (i. 12) expresses it, driven forth by the Spirit into the wilderness to be tempted by Satan. Before beginning His Messianic work, He sought retirement: away from His townsmen of Nazareth and the throngs surrounding the Baptist, He would fix His mind on the nature and means of His enterprise. Here He encountered and overcame those suggestions of the prince of this world, that would have led Him to attempt His work in a selfish, vainglorious, or worldly spirit. He suffered being tempted, yet without sin, for He was full of the Holy Spirit, and had been led to this conflict by the Spirit.

Next we read that He returned in the power of the Spirit (Luke iv. 14) to begin His work of proclaiming and establishing the kingdom of God. Thereafter He speaks of Himself as having the Spirit of God on Him in His teaching (Luke iv. 8), and of casting out demons by the Spirit of God (Matt. xii. 28); and Peter afterwards declared that "God anointed him with the Holy Spirit and with power, who went about doing good and healing all that were oppressed of the devil, for God was with him" (Acts x. 38).

We can hardly doubt also that the great act by which He gave Himself a sacrifice for the sins of men was performed in the power of the Holy Spirit; and this is possibly the meaning of the saying in Heb. ix. 14, that He "through the eternal Spirit offered himself without blemish to God;" although some of the best interpreters prefer to understand the eternal Spirit as His own divine nature. The reference to the Holy Spirit has however a great deal in its favour.

After His resurrection He is still represented as giving commandment to His apostles through the Holy Spirit (Acts i. 2); and thus from first to last His work is described as carried on in the power of the Spirit of God given to Him. This is that anointing which He had for His office, in virtue of which He is the Messiah or Christ, *i.e.* the Anointed One; and this shows us that He is qualified for all the parts of our salvation, not only as God but also as man. He is able perfectly to teach us as a prophet, not merely because He knows all things as God, but because His human mind is enlightened and taught by the Spirit of God: He can appear for us as a great high priest, because He can bear gently with the ignorant and erring, for that He Himself also was compassed with infirmity, and needed the support of the Holy Spirit: He can rule us as a perfect king, because He is not only Almighty God, but our brother, conquering His and our enemies by the power of the Spirit.

Hence, too, when He bestows the Holy Spirit He gives a blessing that He has Himself received and enjoys, and makes us joint-partakers in it with Himself. Thus we read, not only of the gift, but of the communion of the Holy Spirit, *i.e.* partaking in common of the privilege and blessing of having the Spirit of God given to us. It is a fellowship of believers with one another, but also with Christ; they receive the same anointing as He did; it is like the precious ointment on the head of Aaron, that flowed down his beard, and descended even to the skirts of his garments. All the members of our great high priest partake of the anointing of the Holy Spirit, that is given to Him their Head.

This work of the Holy Spirit on Christ affords an explanation of a passage that has caused not a little difficulty to commentators, John xiv. 16, 17: "I will pray the Father, and he shall give you another Comforter, that he may be with you for ever; even the Spirit of truth: whom the world cannot receive, for it beholdeth him not, neither knoweth him: ye know him, for he abideth with you and shall be in you." The gift of the Spirit here promised is future; the disciples received it after our Lord's departure, when so remarkable a change appeared in their whole mental and moral character. How then does Jesus say, "he abideth with you," giving that as the reason why they knew Him? Many understand these statements, though present in form, as future in meaning, so that the sense would be, Ye shall soon know Him, for He shall abide with you. This however is not satisfactory, because the contrast with the world's ignorance, which is undoubtedly present, requires that the disciples' knowledge be present too. Besides, that knowledge is clearly given as the reason why they can receive the Spirit, as the world cannot. It is more in accordance with the force of the words to understand "He abideth with you" as referring to the dwelling of the Spirit in Christ, from which they had come to know Him, though He was not yet in them as He was afterwards to be.[1] The presence of the Spirit of God in Jesus was manifested by His speaking the words of God; as the Baptist said, "He whom God hath sent speaketh the words of God: for he giveth not the Spirit by measure" (John iii. 36); and the disciples had recognised this, when Peter said, "Lord, to whom shall we go? thou hast the

---

[1] This explanation is given by J. C. Hare, *Mission of the Comforter*, pp. 308, 309: "If we make a distinction between the outward and the inward presence of the Spirit, and suppose that the apostles as yet had only enjoyed the former, recognising His power in a measure, as manifested in the life and discourse of their Lord, and being so far enlightened by Him as to discern the divine character of that power, then the promise of the higher gift to them would be in full conformity with that principle, which runs through the whole Scripture, as it does through all the dispensations of life, that to him who has shall be given." In confirmation of this view it may be noticed, that the words rendered "with you" are not the same as in ver. 16. There they mean exactly "along with you;" here, "beside you." On the other hand, however, many weighty authorities read in the last clause of ver. 17 "is in you," for "shall be in you." If that be correct, the interpretation just given must be abandoned. But while the external evidence is pretty equally balanced, internal considerations are in favour of the future tense.

words of eternal life. And we have believed and know that thou art the Holy One of God" (John vi. 68, 69). It was the blindness and sin of the Pharisees that they would not and could not recognise in Jesus' works the agency of the Holy Spirit, but ascribed them to Beelzebub.

In His work on the man Christ Jesus, the Spirit of God is more fully revealed as the Holy Spirit than ever before. Under the Old Testament He had been recognised as the spirit of wisdom and skill in a leader like Moses or an artificer like Bezaleel, as the spirit of strength and courage clothing men like Gideon, Jephthah, Samson, and as the spirit of prophecy in Samuel and his successors: but there had never been seen a perfectly holy man. That was the new thing that appeared in Jesus.

CHAPTER II.

THE SENDING OF THE HOLY SPIRIT BY CHRIST.

JESUS was described by John the Baptist not only as one who had the Holy Spirit dwelling in Him in a manner and fulness that no other man ever had, but also as baptizing with the Holy Spirit (Matt. iii. 11 ; Mark i. 8 ; Luke iii. 16 ; John i. 33). This is what marked Him out as the Messiah, or Founder of the kingdom of God ; for there were numerous prophecies which declared that the reign of Jehovah, that was to bring blessedness to His people, was to be established by the Spirit of God. So Jesus Himself spoke of the Holy Spirit as the best gift of God to men, which as the Heavenly Father He will give to them that ask Him (Luke xi. 13). When He invited all the thirsty to come to Him and drink, and promised to give to every one that believed in Him an abundant supply, so that he should be a well of living water, the evangelist tells us that He spake of the Spirit which they that believed in Him should receive ; and the same evangelist has recorded those farewell discourses in which Jesus promised to send to His disciples another Comforter to supply His place and carry on His work.

Of the fulfilment of these promises there was an outward and visible proof in the events of the day of Pentecost after Jesus' death. But the signs that then appeared to the senses, the sound as of a mighty rushing wind from heaven, the tongues of fire, and even the rapt prophetic utterance of the praises of God by the Galilean disciples of Jesus in strange tongues, formed but the outward and less truly divine side of the event. More truly wonderful was the inward change effected in the disciples and in the people of Jerusalem. In the disciples of Jesus we see a new understanding, a new courage, and a new love: in the multitude an entire revolution of their views and feelings about Jesus.

The disciples had already indeed received some spiritual enlightenment, for they had recognised Jesus as the Messiah, and that not only because of the miracles He did, but because they felt that He had the words of eternal life. They had clung to this faith, even when others were offended by His refusal to accept an earthly crown and by His claim of a heavenly origin. Still they had no idea that it was through suffering and death that He was to enter into His glory; and they looked for places of worldly distinction in His kingdom. They thought He should call down fire from heaven on those who would not receive Him, and even at the last they looked for an immediate restoration of the kingdom to Israel. But on the day of Pentecost we find them proclaiming, that Jesus who had been crucified had entered upon His kingdom, and was really reigning, and no longer do they think of any earthly reign of the Messiah.

But while they thus showed new and enlarged knowledge, the new courage with which they uttered their convictions was still more remarkable. Formerly, when their Master was not with them, they had been timid and inconsistent: in His absence they failed to do works of healing which they attempted; when He set His face to go up to Jerusalem, they were amazed and afraid, and followed Him with fear as to certain death (Mark x. 33; John xi. 8, 16); in His hour of danger all forsook Him and fled, and Peter was ashamed to confess Him even before the maid-servants of the high priest. Even after His resurrection they only ventured to meet with closed doors for fear of the Jews. But on the day of Pentecost they openly declare their faith in Jesus, and boldly accuse the people of the unspeakable guilt of rejecting and crucifying the Messiah, for whom Israel had been looking so long.

There is further manifest in the bearing and discourse of the disciples a wonderful tone of forbearance and love to those who had been the enemies and murderers of their Master. Naturally they might be filled with the bitterest indignation and wrath; and if before they were ready to call down fire from heaven on a Samaritan village simply for not receiving Him on His journey, what threatenings and vengeance might they not be expected to breathe out against the people of Jerusalem who had forced the Roman governor to crucify Him? They do indeed press home on their consciences the awful guilt of their conduct; but they do it evidently more in sorrow than in anger: they do not in the least exaggerate the crime or dwell on its atrocity; they denounce no judgment upon it; they address the guilty people as brethren; they earnestly exhort them to repentance, and cordially convey to them God's promise of forgiveness and the gift of the Holy Spirit if they will but repent. In Peter's speech after the healing of the lame man, he dwells on the fact that their great sin was committed in ignorance, and was overruled by God for the accomplishment of His gracious purpose (Acts iii. 17, 18). In all this there is a tone of generosity, of fellow-feeling, of love, like that of Joseph toward his brethren (Gen. xlv. 5 foll.), yea like that of Jesus Himself, from whom they learned it through the influence of the Holy Spirit.

Such was the spiritual change wrought on those who had already believed in Jesus: it was largely due, no doubt, to the fact of His resurrection, and without that it would be incredible; but they ascribed it also to the influence of the Spirit that Jesus had promised, giving them power to be witnesses for Him.

This Spirit too, according to His promise, wrought on the hearts of those who heard their testimony. The outward sign of their speaking with tongues produced wonder and gained attention to Peter's address; but the address itself carried conviction to the hearts of those who had not many weeks before clamoured for the death of Jesus as a deceiver and blasphemer, and made three thousand willing to enrol themselves as His disciples, though He was still so regarded by the authorities. This too they did under a sense of guilt, and by accepting the rite of baptism, which signified the giving up of their entire past life as polluted, and the acceptance of forgiveness and renewal in the name of Jesus : and they did begin a new life with a love, hope, and joy unknown before, parting with all their goods and casting them into a common stock, and doing all this with alacrity, eating their meat with gladness and joyfulness of heart.

Thus as an actual historical fact the Church of the New Covenant was founded by the Spirit of God sent down from heaven, working in men's hearts as a purifying and animating fire, cleansing them from earthly affections, and warming them with brotherly love and charity : and this renewing influence was given in connection with the testimony of the exaltation of Him who had first taught and shown such holiness and love to men. There are also various indications given, that the connection of the gift of the Holy Spirit with the work of Christ as our Redeemer is peculiarly close and necessary. The fourth evangelist, remarking on Jesus' promise of living water (vii. 39), says "the Spirit was not yet given because Jesus was not yet glorified ; " and he records Jesus' saying (xvi. 7), " If I go not away, the Comforter will not come unto you; but if I go, I will send him unto you." That Jesus' departing and being glorified have special reference to His death appears not only from His sayings in John xii. 23, 24, xiii. 31–33, but from that recorded by Luke xxiv. 49, where, after saying that the Scriptures must needs be fulfilled that the Christ should suffer and rise again from the dead the third day, and that repentance and remission of sins should be preached in His name unto all the nations, he adds : "And behold I send forth the promise of my Father upon you" (compare Acts i. 4, 5, ii. 33). Paul states the connection still more explicitly when he writes to the Galatians, "Christ redeemed us from the curse of the law, having become a curse for us . . . that the blessing of Abraham might come on the Gentiles, that we might receive the promise of the Spirit through faith" (iii. 13, 14); and again,

"God sent forth His Son, made of a woman, made under the law, that He might redeem them that were under the law, that we might receive the adoption of sons. And because ye are sons, God sent forth the Spirit of His Son into your hearts" (iv. 4–6). The principle of this connection is indicated when Paul says that God hath blessed us with all spiritual blessings in Christ; for these blessings include not only redemption and forgiveness, but also the seal and earnest of the Spirit which are all ours in Christ (Eph. i. 3, 7, 13, 14). Sin excludes man from God's blessing, and exposes him to God's wrath and curse, and that implies that God gives over the sinner to his own evil passions (Rom. i. 18, 24, 26, 28). This is the righteous judgment of God, and whatever good is yet bestowed by God on sinners, even His forbearance, not less truly than His forgiveness, is based upon that manifestation of His righteousness made by Christ, whom God hath set forth as a propitiation in His blood through faith (Rom. iii. 24–26). This passage also indicates how these statements of the dependence of the gift of the Spirit on the atoning work of Christ are to be harmonized with the undeniable fact, that the Holy Spirit was bestowed on men in various ways long before Jesus came in the flesh. For it tells us, that His work had a bearing on the passing by of the sins of the past, as well as on the justification of believers at that time and later. As justifying God's gracious dealings with men, it had a retrospective as well as a prospective bearing. Its results were applied by anticipation as it were, because its accomplishment was absolutely certain from the beginning. Hence Jesus, as the spotless Lamb by whose blood we are redeemed, is said to have been foreknown before the foundation of the world (1 Pet. i. 20), and is called the Lamb slain from the foundation of the world (Rev. xiii. 8). As a transaction in the moral government of God the atoning death of Christ has, we may say, no date; it is not conditioned by time at all, but is ever present to the eternal mind of God, as it is also present to our faith, which overleaps the limits of time and place and apprehends a dying Saviour here and now, as often as we look to Him. The dependence of the work of the Holy Spirit on that of Christ is not essentially chronological, but logical and ideal; and so, even when the Spirit was bestowed on men earlier in time than the redemption of Christ was accomplished, it was given on the ground of that redemption as a necessary condition. But as it was designed that the connection should be made manifest, the most signal and abundant effusion of the Spirit was historically after Christ's redemption had become an accomplished fact. Then the Spirit began to exert His gracious influence not only on a few outstanding men in the community, as leaders, prophets, or kings, but on the mass of the people as a whole, and on each single soul among them. Then too the Spirit could work with more power in manifesting to men the love and grace of God, since these had been actually exercised in the highest and most wonderful degree in the life and death of God's Son for sinners. The redemption of Christ is not only the necessary condition, but the appropriate instrument of the Spirit's work. He bears witness of Christ along with the messengers whom He sends (John xv. 26, 27), and when He convinces the world of sin, and of righteousness, and of judgment, it is by making man see what Jesus had done and suffered.

CHAPTER III.

THE WORK OF THE SPIRIT IN THE EXTERNAL CALL OF THE WORD.

WHILE Jesus and His disciples alike teach, in accordance with the intimations of Old Testament prophecy, that the kingdom of God is to be established by the working of His Spirit in the hearts of men ; they declare with equal emphasis that it is also needful that the kingdom be proclaimed, and men called to receive and enter it. The announcement, that the reign of God foretold by the prophets is at hand, is the gospel or glad tidings, that occupies so large and prominent a place in the New Testament; of which Jesus said, "This gospel of the kingdom shall be preached in the whole world for a testimony unto all the nations" (Matt. xxiv. 14) ; of which Paul says, "How shall they believe in him whom they have not heard? and how shall they hear without a preacher?" (Rom. x. 14); and which Peter declares to be "the Word of the Lord which abideth for ever" (1 Pet. i. 25). This proclamation is accompanied with a call to believe and obey the reign of God, or, as it is often expressed, to repentance, that is, to a change of mind and heart, giving up sin as a rebellion against God, trusting in His mercy to forgive it, and returning to our allegiance to Him as our rightful and chosen King.

The importance attached in Scripture to the gospel indicates the general principle, that while God turns us to Himself by the power of His Spirit, He deals with us in accordance with our nature, as creatures possessing reason and free-will. He does not move men to faith and obedience by the same kind of power by which He guides the planets in their courses, or bring back wandering prodigals by laws such as those that bring comets from the depths of space back to their central sun. Neither does He move them by any mere blind overpowering instinct, like those by which "the stork in the heaven knoweth her appointed times, and the turtle and the swallow and the crane observe the time of their coming:" He addresses a call to their understanding, their conscience, their affections, and their will; and brings all these powers of the soul into action, when He creates them anew in Christ Jesus unto good works.

This call of the gospel, however, derives its power, even as an external invitation, from its being the call of God Himself, and not merely of our fellow-men. It comes to us indeed through our fellow-men, and it is accompanied with their earnest advice and entreaty to comply with it; but if it is to warrant and encourage us to come to God as penitent sinners, trusting His mercy, we must have the assurance that it really expresses the mind and will of God Himself. Now that which gives us this assurance in connection with the gospel call, is that work of the Holy Spirit which is commonly called inspiration, the effect of which is, that we can regard the Scriptures of the Old and New Testaments as the Word of God written, and our infallible rule of faith and life.

Moses and the prophets of Israel, who as we have seen were moved by the Spirit of God, spoke in His name, saying, "Thus saith the Lord," and so their utterances were the Word of God. The earlier prophets wrought chiefly by speech and action, as Samuel, Nathan, Elijah, and Elisha, who have left no written records of their prophecies; but the history of Israel was written in the prophetic spirit in a series of books regarded by the Hebrews as divine, and called "the former prophets;" and these were followed by a collection of the works of the inspired men, who committed their discourses to writing, "the later prophets." These, together with the five books of the Law, giving Israel's divine legislation set in the history of the people from the beginning, and with a collection called Scriptures, or holy writings (*Kethubhim, Hagiographa*), including the Psalms, the Solomonic writings, and others of later date, constituted the sacred books of Israel. Though some questions as to its precise limits were discussed by the Rabbis at and after our Lord's time, in general the collection was recognised as the written Word of God from a much earlier date; and the Law and the Prophets were regularly read in the synagogues as divine. In moral and spiritual character these books show a very marked superiority to later Jewish religious writings, some of which were mixed with them in the Greek translation of the LXX., and having been used as Scripture by some of the early Christians, were put by the Council of Trent on a level with the books of Scripture.

The actual words of Jesus, the incarnate Son of God, who spoke as one having authority, and not as the scribes, are doubtless in the most direct sense the Word of God. Even in these, as we have seen, the agency of the Spirit is to be recognised. But Jesus acknowledged the absolute authority of the Old Testament Scripture as divine, and on a perfect level with His own words; and on one occasion at least, when appealing to it as such, He indicated that it was the agency of the Spirit that gave it that character; when reasoning with the scribes as to the dignity of the expected Messiah, He asked, "How doth David in the Spirit (or in the Holy Spirit) call him Lord?" (Matt. xxii. 43; Mark xii. 36).

Jesus also intimated, that what He actually said with His own lips did not constitute the whole of what He had to teach His disciples; for He had many things to say to them, which they could not bear, even at the very end of His personal training of them (John xvi. 12); but He promised that the Spirit, being the Spirit of truth, would guide them into all the truth, for He should speak at Jesus' command and unfold to them the things of Jesus, which include all that the Father hath. These words, as they indicate distinctly a completion by the Spirit of the teaching of Jesus, seem to denote not merely that gracious enlightenment of the Spirit which is common to all believers, and to which most of His sayings in this discourse refer, but a special divine influence, that would make what was said or written under it as truly the Word of God as the Law and the Prophets, and the discourses of Jesus Himself. Accordingly we find that there were in the early Church prophets (Acts xiii. 1; Rom. xii. 6; 1 Cor. xii. xiv.), whose gifts are ascribed to the Holy Spirit. The disciples from the day of Pentecost onwards were filled with the Holy Spirit, and spoke with authority in the name of God; and their words, like those of the Old Testament prophets, were often attested by miraculous signs to confirm their authority. Similar authority is claimed for what they wrote in the form of epistles for the instruction and confirmation of their converts. Paul, who was probably the first to adopt this plan, says: "If any man think himself to be a prophet or spiritual, let him acknowledge, that the things that I write unto you are the commandments of the Lord" (1 Cor. xiv. 37); and in the other epistles of the New Testament there is a similar tone of authority. One book, the Apocalypse, is in form and substance prophetic, and records visions asserted to have been received in the Spirit (Rev. i. 10); and while the writers of the Gospels and Acts refer sometimes to their human means of knowledge, and make no express claim to divine inspiration, they give forth their records as possessing a certainty that may be the ground of saving faith (Luke i. 4; John xx. 31). The collection of the New Testament as a whole has the same marks of moral and spiritual excellence, as compared with the immediately following Christian literature, as the Old Testament has in comparison with later Jewish religious writings.

Thus, through the agency of the Holy Spirit, there has been composed a volume which is entitled to be called the Word of God. The nature of the inspiration by which this has been effected is, like every operation of the Spirit of God, mysterious; and as this work in particular is not, like His converting and sanctifying agency, one of which all Christians have experience, it is on this account also impossible of explanation. We can only know its results; and these are twofold. On the one hand, what is thus written possesses absolute authority as a message from God; for if Jesus was content to bow with implicit submission to the saying, "It is written," how much rather should we? On the other hand, the teaching of the Spirit of God comes to us through men of like nature to ourselves, whose faculties have not been superseded, but used, by the inspiration of the Spirit. It is therefore intelligible to us; and its meaning can be correctly ascertained by the rules by which ordinary human writings are interpreted. The inspired writers use the language of their country and of their time with perfect freedom, fall into grammatical and rhetorical irregularities; do not display literary perfection of style; employ the customary liberty of disregarding minute accuracy of detail where that would be needless or out of place; and adopt popular views on matters of science and history. They have each his own character, not only in style, but in the views of truth which they present, and sometimes apparently contradict, while they really supplement each other. A complete view of revealed truth is only to be obtained by comparing and combining all their lights; but each portion of the Word, when read in the light of its connection, has some message from God to men.

In virtue of this work of inspiration, the Holy Scripture is the Word of God, and more especially of the Holy Spirit; and passages from it are quoted by Jesus and His apostles as spoken by God (Matt. xix. 4, 5), or by the Holy Spirit (Acts xxviii. 25; Heb. iii. 8, ix. 8; 1 Pet. i. 11), and sometimes the Scripture is said to speak, when the meaning is that God speaks by the Scripture (John xix. 37; Gal. iii. 8). To Scripture therefore belongs supreme authority; and to it is due absolute deference, as the Word of God and infallible rule of faith and practice. God's revelation of Himself in Jesus Christ for our salvation, having been thus committed to writing, enables each one of us to hear His voice speaking to ourselves, without being dependent on the intervention of any human priest or prophet. We may indeed be greatly helped by the knowledge, wisdom, and teaching of our brethren ; but we are never in a position in which we absolutely need them to tell us what is the mind and will of God concerning us; we may through the Scriptures learn that from God Himself, and be sure that God is speaking to us, and that we hear His voice. Indeed, as long as we know the truth, however fully and correctly, only from the teaching of others, we know nothing as we ought to know ; if we would really hear and obey the Word of God, we must read the Bible for ourselves, to be convinced that it is the Word of God, and perceive its real meaning. That we may be able to do so, the Scripture possesses a self-evidencing and self-interpreting power, which makes it independent of external testimony and explanation. Its self-evidencing power, or internal evidence, consists chiefly in its efficacy to enlighten the mind, awaken the conscience, and draw the heart towards God. This power belongs in substance to the matter of Scripture, the gospel embodied in it, and is felt also when that is faithfully presented in uninspired speech or writing; but it is found in a special degree as the gospel is received in the original form and with the direct authority which it has in Scripture. The self-interpreting power or perspicuity of Scripture arises from the fact that it is written by men like ourselves, the Holy Spirit using not only their lips and pens, but their minds, their imaginations, their feelings ; so that by a natural unstrained interpretation, in accordance with the common rules of language, we reach the real meaning. Had Scripture been a series of oracles like those that human superstition has imagined, dictated by the Deity without the intervention of a human mind, its interpretation would have been arbitrary and ambiguous, and there would have been need of some authoritative interpreter to guide us to its real meaning ; but since it is truly human as well as divine, its import can be clearly and certainly ascertained. Since indeed it was given at sundry times and in divers manners, some of its parts are not so easily intelligible as others ; but a variety of form and style was necessary for a book intended for all men in all ages;

and this very variety, as it presents the same truths in different points of view, affords, when carefully studied, the better means of making sure that we understand them aright.

In regard to its contents, the Scripture, thus written by men inspired by the Holy Spirit, so as to convey to us the Word of God, is a unity, having for its one great subject the grace of God bringing salvation, which has appeared to all men in Jesus Christ. He said Himself of the Scriptures which the Jews searched, "These are they that testify of me" (John v. 39). Paul says, that the glad tidings of God concerning His Son, unto which he was separated, had been promised before by His prophets in the holy scriptures (Rom. i. 2); and an angel declares in the Apocalyptic vision, "The testimony of Jesus is the spirit of prophecy" (Rev. xix. 10) Because this salvation is a historical salvation, accomplished under fit conditions of place, time, and preparation, the message about it is set in a history, and largely embodied in historical records : because it is a holy salvation, its announcement is accompanied with instructions and precepts of holiness ; but the centre and sum of the Word of God is the joyful message of God's mercy and grace to sinners through Jesus Christ, with the invitation and command to all men to accept it as freely offered to them.

This is the external call by which God turns sinners to Himself : it is conveyed to us by the work of the Holy Spirit inspiring the writers of Scripture ; and this outward call of the Word, not the inward work of the Spirit in our hearts, is the ground and warrant of our faith. It is our duty to believe and accept God's grace in Christ, simply because He testifies and offers it to us in the gospel, whether or not we experience any working of His Spirit in our hearts. The external call is well fitted to form a ground of our faith, because of the qualities that belong to it.

It is gracious, proceeding from God's free undeserved mercy and love to men, not due in justice or equity. We are told that God spared not the angels that sinned, but cast them down to hell (2 Pet. ii. 4 ; Jude 6) ; and that He taketh not hold of angels to save them (Heb. ii. 16); and in perfect justice He might have dealt so with men; but in His sovereign mercy He has "so loved the world, that he gave his only-begotten Son, that whosoever believeth in him should not perish, but have eternal life." Both the salvation itself and the offer of it are therefore entirely of free grace; and the offer is unfettered by any condition, to be had simply for the taking, that is by faith, without money and without price.

Again, God's call in the gospel is sincere: God is in earnest in making it; and it expresses His real and sincere desire that all men should be saved and come to the knowledge of the truth (1 Tim. ii. 4). He declares in the most solemn terms, condescending even to confirm it with an oath, that He has no pleasure at all in the death of the wicked, but that the wicked should turn from his wickedness and live (Ezek. xxxiii. 11); He "is long-suffering to us-ward, not willing that any should perish, but that all should come to repentance" (2 Pet. iii. 9). True, it is a firm principle of His kingdom, that except men repent they shall all perish; and He will execute judgment on all who obey not the gospel of His Son: but if any perish, it is not because God has any pleasure in that, or has made it necessary, but because they would not repent and believe the gospel. If any will not do so, God will certainly and justly punish them; but oh, how much rather would He have them believe and live!

Further, the gospel call is universal, addressed to men as such, and therefore to all men without exception and without distinction; not to any one nation or class, but to all; not to the civilized, or the moral, or the awakened, or the earnest, but to all alike, to the most degraded and worst of sinners, as truly as to the most enlightened and earnest seekers after God. True, it is not actually made known to all men in the world; but whose fault is that? Not God's; for He has sent a Saviour for all, and given His disciples a commission to go into all the world and make disciples of all nations. Had they been faithful to their charge, and had men been as anxious to receive, and as ready to welcome the gospel as Christ was to send it, long ere now every human being would have heard it. But many to whom this gracious message came refused and rejected it, persecuted and slew its preachers; and the efforts of Christians were discouraged; and their faith and love grew cold; and they ceased to seek to evangelize the world. It is to these and similar causes, all arising from the unbelief and sin of man, that it is due, that the gospel has not been actually proclaimed to all men, not to anything that God has done.

Once more, the gospel call is powerful, because not only has the Scripture as inspired by the Holy Spirit an intrinsic might and efficacy, but the same Spirit also accompanies the Word with a direct work on the souls of those who hear it. The Spirit of God accompanies the outward call of the gospel with an inward call, by which the Word is brought home to the consciences and hearts of men; so that it is not only heard but understood, and in some measure felt, in its commanding authority and persuasive grace. Thus the gospel that is addressed to all men through the Word, which the Holy Spirit has inspired and accompanies with His convincing influence, is sufficient to render those who hear it inexcusable if they do not obey it. Being gracious, sincere, universal, and made intelligible and appreciable by all, it affords ample motive and warrant for faith; and if men were only willing to receive it, there is nothing whatever to prevent them. Since God has provided such a salvation, and made such an offer of it to sinners, if any who hear it are not saved, the blame of this cannot be laid on God, but must be ascribed entirely to themselves. God is willing and earnestly desirous that they should be saved through Christ; but they will not come to Christ that they may have life.

CHAPTER IV.

THE WORK OF THE SPIRIT IN CONVICTION.

THE work of the Holy Spirit on all those who hear the gospel deserves more particular consideration, as it affords a link of connection between those of His operations which are entirely external to the believer, as His work on Christ and His inspiration of the Scriptures, and those that are carried on in the believer's own soul in his conversion, sanctification, instruction, and consolation. By the inspiration of Holy Scripture, the Spirit makes the message conveyed in it to be really the Word of God; and by His work of conviction, accompanying the preaching of the Word, He secures that it is known and felt by the hearers to be God's Word to them. Without this it could have no power either to convince the mind that it is really the mind of God, or to overcome the misgivings of an evil conscience, or the alienation of a selfish and worldly heart from God. But the Spirit of God makes a direct communication between God and the soul of man; so that the gospel as it comes to us is really known and felt to be the Word of God (see 1 Thess. ii. 13, cf. i. 5), not merely men speaking to us about God, but God Himself speaking to our souls. Paul seems to indicate that this is the difference between those cases in which the gospel is ineffectual, and those in which it leads to a new faith and life: and is it not really so? There are many who know the great truths of Christianity, and often hear its lessons enforced, yet show no appearance of that new life that Paul ascribes to the faith of the gospel. They do not disbelieve the truths they hear; but they receive them merely as what their ministers tell them, or what divines have drawn from the Bible, without any sense or idea that God Himself is speaking to them. Can we wonder that the gospel produces little or no effect on them? It is when men are brought face to face with God, as He has come near to us in Jesus Christ, that they are really influenced by His Word.

Now it is by His Spirit, as we have already seen, that God comes into direct contact with man : the human spirit as breathed into man by God at the first, is akin to the divine, and the Spirit of God has access to that of man. Hence even the earthly ministry of Jesus Himself the Son of God could not effectually win the hearts of men, save through the Spirit of God. He indeed perfectly revealed the Father, and in His cross revealed Him as forgiving sins, a just God and a Saviour; but it was needful that He should depart in bodily presence and come by the Spirit, that men might be brought to turn to the Father in penitence, love, and obedience. But it is by revealing Christ as the image of God to the inmost soul of man, that the Spirit of God works; He glorifies Christ, for He takes of His, and shows it to men, and that which is Christ's includes all that the Father hath (John xvi. 14, 15). So also Paul teaches that the Spirit reveals Christ in us, and enables us to call Him Lord, and to see in Him the glory of God, so as to be conformed to the same image (Gal. i. 16; 1 Cor. ii. 10-16, xii. 3; 2 Cor. iii. 3, 18, iv. 6).

What is meant by this may be understood if we consider how God is known by man. While there are undoubtedly evidences of the being and attributes of God in His works, that appeal to the understanding, and that can be exhibited, as they often have been, in the form of arguments; there is reason to think, that these seldom have been the earliest means of leading men to believe that God is, but that they have first come to this belief through the sense of the absolute authority of the law of duty, and of the reverence and obedience due to it. They feel themselves under law, and therefore under a Supreme Lawgiver and Judge. Thus first do we come into any personal relation to God.

But the moral sense, as we know, is very apt to be blunted and vitiated. When pleasure or self-love prevails over the dictates of duty, it becomes painful to listen to the voice of conscience, and so attention is turned away from it ; and by disuse the delicacy of its discernment is blunted, and the authority with which it speaks is forgotten. Thus it comes to pass that the true knowledge of God is lost, because the faculty by which it is received is disordered ; and if men in this state still go on thinking and arguing about God, they are led farther and farther into error. They have no true understanding of His character, or His will, or His works; and this is what is meant by the mind being blinded, and unable to apprehend spiritual things.

Now when the mind is in this state, and both Scripture and experience declare, that the minds of all men are by nature in such a state, there is needed, in order to their enlightenment, not only the presentation of objects of knowledge, but the restoration of the power of knowing in the mind itself. There must therefore be, not merely the proclamation of the gospel to the mind, but some work on or in the mind, enabling it to see that this is indeed a message from God, and to perceive its meaning. This is the enlightening or convincing work of the Holy Spirit.

Yet this work is not the creation of a new faculty entirely absent before ; it is the restoration of power to a faculty that had become blind and impotent by disuse. Now the analogy of nature teaches us, that in such cases the power is to be restored by using it so far as it remains. The faculty of moral discernment is there, though in regard to God and the things of God it has lost its power. That power must be restored by the exercise of the faculty on what it can discern. So, for example, when David had been living in sin, untouched with any sense of its evil, Nathan opened his eyes to see that, by presenting, in the parable of the ewe lamb, a case in which he still could judge correctly, and by calling him to judge in this case, enabled him to judge himself.

In like manner, the Spirit opens the eyes of men to see their real relation to God, and their moral state in His sight, by setting these things before them in such a palpable way that they can discern them. "When he is come," said Jesus, "he shall convince the world of sin, and of righteousness, and of judgment; of sin, because they believe not in me, of righteousness because I go to the Father and ye see me no more, of judgment because the prince of this world is judged." These convictions are to be brought home to men through their knowledge of the life and work of Jesus; and the way in which this is done is shown by the record in the Book of Acts, of the fulfilment of that promise. The gift of the Holy Spirit to the disciples of Jesus on the day of Pentecost was set forth as a proof of His resurrection (Acts ii. 32, 33); and that again was evidence that He was Lord and Messiah (Acts ii. 36). Their unbelief therefore, the guilt of which they had not moral discernment to perceive in itself, now appeared to them as crucifying their Messiah and King; and when they heard that, they were pricked in their hearts, and said, "What shall we do?" (Acts ii. 37). The Holy Spirit was convincing them of sin, inasmuch as He was manifestly working in the disciples of Jesus, and so presenting to the Jews the sin of their conduct in a way in which they could not but see it.

This, we may believe, was the use of the outward miracles that accompanied the preaching of the gospel, and also many of God's earlier messages. They presented to the dull and hardened minds of men broad outlines and bright colours which they could discern; and by thus calling their moral judgment into exercise, made it capable of perceiving truths to which at first it was blind. But the same purpose is served, more extensively and not less effectually, by those graces and virtues of the Christian life which are the fruits of the Spirit as truly and unmistakably as the extraordinary gifts that have now ceased. These serve to convey to the minds of ignorant and prejudiced men conceptions of spiritual and divine things formerly strange to them. For example, a missionary goes to preach the gospel of Christ to the savage tribes of Central Africa, or the South Sea Islands: he tells them of the love of God to men; but they cannot take it in; they have no such feeling in their own hearts, and they can form no idea of what it is. But he lives among them, shows them kindness, bears patiently with their hostility, heals them in sickness, saves them from death; and they gradually come to see what love is, and recognising the love of man, they are led to believe the love of God. Then too they will come to see the moral evil of their inhumanity, and ingratitude, and vice; and thus their minds will be enlightened, and their consciences convinced of sin. So in other cases an inability to understand Christian doctrine may be removed, in accordance with the laws of our mental nature, by the presentation of the reality of Christian life; and this is the work of the Holy Spirit acting indirectly on the world.

In this sense Christ's disciples are the light of the world: having received light from Him, they reflect it on others. They have been raised to the position of a city set on a hill, where the light of the Sun of righteousness shines. The world is in the valley below, where that light is not seen directly; but men can see it reflected from the city that cannot be hid, and may thus be persuaded to come up thither. "Let your light," said Jesus, "so shine among men, that they may see your good works and glorify your Father which is in heaven" (Matt. v. 16). So the same work of conviction, that is ascribed by Christ to the Spirit, is assigned by Paul to Christians, as having been once darkness but now light in the Lord. "Have no fellowship with the unfruitful works of darkness, but rather even reprove them. . . . But all things when they are reproved are made manifest by the light" (Eph. v. 11-13). But this conviction and illumination is also ascribed to Christ (v. 14). Christ works through His Spirit in His own people, presenting Christianity to the world in such a way that men come to see things to which they were formerly blind, and to feel convictions to which they were before insensible.

This is the reason why our Catechism says, that the Holy Spirit maketh "the reading, but especially the preaching, of the word an effectual means of convincing and converting sinners." The preaching of the word, according to Christ's appointment, is the proclamation of it by a man who feels its truth and preciousness, who is influenced by its power and trusts its promises. Hence in such preaching the word is accompanied by the living personality of a Christian man, and so the reality of Christian life is presented along with the verbal declaration of it ; and the spiritual power of preaching lies greatly in the personality of the preacher as a man of God.

We are not indeed to suppose, that it is only through His work in Christians that the Holy Spirit enlightens and convinces the world. He may exercise some direct influence upon them, though of the nature of that we can form no distinct conception ; and He does work often by the Word alone, and makes it the means of giving light to those blinded by prejudice and sin. Indeed, there is reason to believe that the gospel is never unaccompanied with this work of the Spirit ; and that all the convictions, relentings, misgivings, desires, and aspirations that are felt under the preaching of the gospel, are due, not merely to the truth in itself, nor to the eloquence of the preacher, but to the working of the Holy Spirit. That this is so appears from the familiar facts, that the same truths often have very different effects, not only on different persons, but on the same person at different times, so that what at one time we hear with indifference, at another time stirs us with emotion to the very depths of our soul ; and that it is not always the most eloquent preachers who have been most blessed in the awakening and conversion of souls. In the way in which men are convinced of sin and awakened to see religious truth under the preaching of the gospel, there is something more than can be accounted for by the ordinary principles of logic and rhetoric : the Bible leads us to ascribe this to the Spirit of God ; and we have seen that if we recognise such an agent working in the hearts of men, the facts of experience are sufficiently and naturally accounted for. God is awakening into exercise faculties dormant or diseased by disuse, in a way analogous to that in which such a process ordinarily goes on.

This work of the Spirit, however, is one that may be resisted and overcome, and does not always lead to conversion. There is in the natural heart of man a tendency to resist it; for the convictions which it produces are very humbling and painful. It dispels the self-complacency in which men may have been indulging, thinking that they are tolerably virtuous, or at least not worse than others; it awakens them to a sense of ungodliness and unbrotherliness; it shows them that they ought to make a most humiliating confession of sin to God, and a most thorough change of heart and life. To this their pride, their selfishness, their indolence and love of ease, are strongly opposed; and these sometimes induce men to put away from them the unwelcome message, and to stifle the inward conviction of its truth. They may put off the consideration of the claims of Christianity, and plunge into the business or pleasures of the world; or they may set themselves in violent opposition to the gospel, and endeavour to persuade themselves that it is not true; and in some such way it often happens that convictions that were once serious and seemed to be deep pass away.

When this takes place, the result is, that the heart becomes hardened until it may at last be entirely insensible and unimpressible even by the most powerful and touching appeals. This is in accordance with two general laws of our mental and moral nature. One is, that impressions in which the soul is passive, when they are not yielded to, become more and more feeble, until at length they may cease to produce any effect at all. In this way, those who hear the gospel at first with much feeling, and seem to be almost persuaded to comply with it, but yet refuse or delay to do so, will hear it again with less emotion; and if they continue to disobey the call, they may come to such a state, that they cannot feel the power of the truths that once impressed them so deeply. Such impressions are therefore not to be trifled with. They are precious and useful as helps towards conversion, and may greatly promote our spiritual life, if they are cherished and obeyed ; but their continuance cannot be counted on ; and if they are neglected, they will disappear and give place to utter hardness of heart. But this is not all ; for since, according to the law of habit, while passive impressions become feebler, active efforts become stronger by repetition, the effort that the ungodly mind must make to shake off impressions that are strongly made by the gospel tends, every time it is made, to become easier and more likely. Thus by a twofold process, perfectly in accordance with the ordinary course of nature, the gospel becomes to those who refuse it a means of hardening, not as it is intended to be, of conversion. This effect of the unbelieving hearing of the divine call is often spoken of in Scripture ; and as it may end when it runs its full course in utter and hopeless hardness of heart, this is probably the explanation of the solemn and mysterious statements by our Lord and His apostles about blasphemy against the Holy Spirit, as a sin that has no forgiveness (Matt. xii. 31, 32; Mark iii. 28, 29 ; Luke xii. 10), the sin unto death (1 John v. 16, 17), the wilful apostasy, from which it is impossible to renew men again to repentance (Heb. vi. 4–6, x. 26–29). When we compare with these sayings the plain and repeated statements of revelation, that Jesus Christ came into the world to save sinners even the chief, that His blood cleanses from all sin, that all men, even the most guilty, are assured of forgiveness, if they repent and believe in Jesus ; we perceive that this sin is not unpardonable because of its great or peculiar guilt, but because by its nature it makes repentance and faith impossible. Hence it is not so much a definite or particular offence, as a certain frame of mind, or manner of sinning ; and it is mentioned in Scripture in the obscure way that has sometimes caused perplexity, for this practical reason, that the purpose of revelation is not to make us anxiously cautious against one special sin, while comparatively careless about others ; but to make us hate and resist all sin, and feel the evil and danger even of the least ; since there is no form of sin, however apparently trifling, that if indulged, may not lead to that which is unto death. There is no sin that appears to worldly men more light and trivial than that of unbelief; yet nothing approaches nearer to a description of the sin against the Holy Spirit than persistent and final unbelief. Thus we have constant need to be saying with the Psalmist, "Who can understand his errors? Cleanse thou me from secret faults, keep back thy servant also from presumptuous sins. So shall I be upright, and I shall be innocent from the great transgression" (Ps. xix. 12, 13).

CHAPTER V.

THE WORK OF THE HOLY SPIRIT IN CONVERSION.

THE gracious call of the gospel of Christ is universal, addressed to sinners of mankind as such, and to all men alike, and is a result and evidence of God's philanthropy (Tit. iii. 4), or love to men, and earnest desire that all men should be saved and come to the knowledge of the truth. This is further confirmed by that awakening, enlightening, and convincing work of the Spirit that accompanies the proclamation of the gospel. But all do not believe in Jesus as offered in the gospel; and many who experience convictions wrought by the Spirit of God, resist and stifle these and become hardened in impenitence and sin; while others are brought to repentance and faith in Jesus Christ. What is the cause of the difference? In the case of those who continue in sin, this result must be ascribed entirely to themselves. All that God does tends to lead them to repentance: He has sent a Saviour who is both able and willing to save them; He sincerely invites and urges them to come to Him that they may have life; He awakens them by His Spirit to a sense of their sin and misery, and pricks them in their consciences and hearts. If they will not turn to Him, it is because their weak self-love and guilty pride hinder them; not because God puts any obstacles in their way; and if God is said sometimes to harden their hearts, He does so because of their wilful unbelief, and that simply by leaving them to themselves as they desire; He endures in great long-suffering vessels of wrath fitted, by themselves, for destruction; and they become hardened under the very means that God uses to soften others. This simply means, that God does not interfere with the laws of our mental and moral nature, according to which impressions disregarded become more and more feeble, while actions repeated become habits, and habits indulged acquire the strength and persistency of a second nature.

But on the other hand, when men are led to faith in Christ, this is not due to their own will, but to the grace of God. So the Bible uniformly represents it; and so all earnest Christians have practically acknowledged. The will is indeed exercised in the act of faith and repentance; it is a voluntary act by which the soul turns from sin and trusts in Jesus Christ as the Saviour of sinners. But this act it is moved and enabled to perform by the influence of the grace of God. Jesus asserts in the most emphatic manner the absolute necessity of being born from above in order to enter or even see the kingdom of God (John iii. 3, 5, 7, 8); and Paul describes those who believe as having been dead in sins, and as quickened to a new life by a power as great as that which raised Christ from the dead (Eph. ii. 1–10). James (i. 18) describes them as brought forth of God's will by the word of truth; Peter (1 Pet. i. 23), as begotten again of incorruptible seed by the word of God; and John, as begotten of God (1 John ii. 29, iv. 7, v. 1). The same thing is indicated by the promises that God will circumcise the heart (Deut. xxx. 6), give a new heart and a right spirit (Ezek. xxxvi. 26, 27), write His laws in the heart (Jer. xxxi. 31–34), and the like.

Christian experience seems to show that this is done in connection with very different forms of consciousness in different cases. Sometimes the great change seems to be sudden and abrupt, as in the conversion of Paul; sometimes, while there has been a long and gradual preparation for it, the change at the last is decisive and clearly marked, as in the case of Augustine; while in other instances the process may be so steady and gradual that no distinct transition can be marked at all. Yet in all cases it is found, that the purpose and will of the Christian life has to contend against opposing and downward tendencies in the soul,—tendencies which we can see, either in an earlier stage of the same life, or in other lives, have unresisted sway, and draw men down to utter selfishness and worldliness. These downward tendencies prevail wherever men are left to themselves without the elevating influence of the grace of God in Christ; and they sometimes overcome even the moral influence of that grace, and the convictions awakened by the Holy Spirit in connection with the gospel of Christ. The presence of these downward tendencies, even in the souls of those who have from their earliest days of conscious life been seeking God, and can trace no definite beginning of religion in their hearts, convinces them, that however early they have come to strive upwards, it has been not of themselves, but by God's drawing that they have done so. Scripture teaches that God can and does sometimes bestow His Holy Spirit on men from their very birth; but even when there is reason to think He has done so, there is evidence that the goodness that begins so early is due, not to their own nature, but to God's grace.

In these cases, the grace of God is most clearly seen to be, as theologians have called it, prevenient, *i.e.* going before any efforts of man after goodness, and really calling these into exercise. But this is not less true in all cases. The renewal of the soul cannot be traced to any uniform antecedent on the part of man. Sometimes indeed it may seem to be the result of earnest desire and strenuous effort after holiness or peace of mind; but in many other cases, it is effected where there has been no such previous desire, and sinners are arrested in the full course of worldliness and vice. Sometimes, again, it may seem as if the very force and earnestness of character, that makes some men plunge recklessly into evil, was a preparation for their being as earnest and thoroughgoing in good, when once the call of Christ is presented to them. But there are many, on the other hand, whose very failing has been weakness and indecision of purpose, but who have been laid hold of by the power of the gospel and made decided and earnest in faith. In like manner, a profoundly emotional nature, like that of Augustine, may sometimes appear to explain why a man is converted; but there are many other cases of conversion, in which nothing of that kind can be traced. This is a great encouragement to all who are earnestly desirous to have the life of Christ in them, but may be in doubt or anxiety whether what they experience is really the renewing work of the Spirit, and may fear that they are not earnest enough, or not susceptible enough, or have not enough depth of spiritual nature, to be really converted and born again. It is reassuring to know, that the new birth does not depend on any such conditions, but on the free grace of God, who is often found of those who seek Him not, but never allows any to seek Him in vain. He shows His sovereignty, not in the way of denying the gracious influence of His Spirit to any who desire it, but in bestowing it on many who desire it not, or even strongly oppose it; while in other cases, he leaves to their own devices those who obstinately resist that work of His Spirit that is common to all. The general rule of the bestowal of His grace is that they who seek shall find: it is never less than that; but oftentimes it is much more, and they who seek not are found of God, and even those whose selfish and worldly will is strongly set against Him are often arrested in their downward course, awakened to serious thought, and turned to God.

How this is done consistently with the freedom of their will, is indeed a profound mystery. When we consider the statements of Scripture describing the work of the Holy Spirit in conversion as a new creation, a quickening and raising from the dead, a begetting again; and when we observe how the most vehement and persistent opponents of Christianity have often been transformed into sincere and fervent believers, we cannot doubt that the Holy Spirit does exert a power which changes the natural current of the affections, and overcomes the obstinacy of the evil heart. Yet no violence is done to the will of those who are thus converted : their choice is not coerced by irresistible force ; nor is their reason overpowered by uncontrollable passion : they have the full exercise of all their faculties; and they repent and accept Christ as their Saviour and Lord freely and willingly. The renewing work of the Spirit of God is in a region beneath the sphere of consciousness ; and so it must ever remain hidden in itself, though it is made clearly manifest by its results. We know that we are subject to many influences of which we have no consciousness or direct knowledge. We inherit certain characters from our parents ; we are affected by the unconscious influence of friends, of society, of the spirit of the times ; some of these causes may transform our habits and course of conduct ; and we may be quite sensible of the change that has taken place, though we cannot explain it; we feel that it has not been due to our own will, while yet it has done no violence to our freedom. These are indeed merely analogies ; and we cannot but regard the influence of the Spirit of God as more deep and lasting than any of these earthly and human influences ; but when we see that the freedom of the soul is not infringed by any of these, powerful as they are, we may have less difficulty in believing that the soul may be turned to God by an almighty influence of His Spirit, while yet it turns freely, being made willing by His grace.

We speak of the influence of the Spirit in conversion as almighty ; and we are warranted to do so by the way in which it is spoken of in Scripture, and by the very fact that the Holy Spirit is divine. But we must remember that this work is not in the material, but in the moral sphere; and therefore the omnipotence we ascribe to it is not that of physical force but of moral and spiritual influence. The power by which a sinner is turned from the world to God is not of the same kind as that by which the Red Sea was divided or Jordan turned back before Israel : it is not merely the divine will working on nature : it is the power of truth working on the mind, of duty affecting the conscience, and above all of infinite grace, melting and moving the heart. The certain and effectual working of it is expressed in such utterances as these: "Lord, to whom shall we go? Thou hast the words of eternal life" (John vi. 68); "The love of Christ constraineth us" (2 Cor. v. 14). Thus, while it is certainly effectual, it is not harsh, violent, or overbearing; but sweet, gentle, and loving: it is, as Augustine called it, "victorious delight;" as the Synod of Dort described it, "most powerful and at the same time most sweet;" or as Dr. Chalmers put it, "the expulsive power of a new affection."

The terms regeneration and conversion, which are both used for this work of the Spirit, ought in strict accuracy to be distinguished; and some important practical ends are served by the distinction. Sometimes indeed they may be used interchangeably. Thus Jesus said on one occasion (Matt. xviii. 3), "Except ye turn (or be converted), and become as little children, ye shall in no wise enter into the kingdom of heaven;" and on another occasion (John iii. 3), "Except a man be born anew, he cannot see the kingdom of God;" and the meaning is substantially the same. But from the use of the word conversion, and its cognate verb in other places, we find that it is equivalent to repentance and faith. In Acts iii. 19 conversion is enjoined along with repentance, either as a fuller description of what repentance means, or as the change of conduct that follows the change of mind; and in Acts xv. 3 the conversion of the Gentiles is used to describe their faith in Christ (xiii. 48, xiv. 23, 27). In the same sense the word is employed in Matt. xiii. 15, John xii. 40, and Acts xxviii. 27. Further, it is not limited to the first acts of faith and repentance, by which one becomes a Christian, though it is more frequently used of them; but is also employed for the restoration of a backslider (Luke xxii. 32; Jas. v. 19, 20). Thus it describes a moral change in which man is conscious and active, though he is also moved by the Spirit of God, and one that must be continued, and may often be renewed in the course of the Christian life. Regeneration, on the other hand, is never identified with the conscious acts of faith and repentance; but is distinguished from faith as its cause (John i. 12, 13; 1 John v. 1). So too the good works that are the fruits of faith and repentance are described by Paul as proceeding from the act of God quickening the soul that had been dead in sin (Eph. ii. 4–10).

Conversion is thus the act of the new spiritual life, more especially its first act or beginning; but regeneration is the implanting of the new life by God; and so it is also called a quickening, or making alive, a raising from the dead, a new creation, the giving a new heart. This comes first in the order of nature, though in time both may be contemporaneous. If we take Paul's figure of a resurrection, and compare the quickening of the dead soul to Jesus' raising Lazarus from the grave; regeneration corresponds to the supernatural act by which life was imparted to the dead body, and conversion to his coming out of the tomb in the exercise of that restored life. Both alike were connected with the voice of Jesus, when He cried with a loud voice, "Lazarus, come forth;" and thus regeneration and conversion are associated with the call of the gospel to sinners to believe and repent; but just as that voice would have had no power to raise the dead had it not been uttered by Him whom the Father heareth always, and who is Himself the resurrection and the life; so the gospel call cannot of itself turn men to God, unless it come not in word only, but in power, and in the Holy Spirit (1 Thess. i. 5). The connection of the call of the gospel with conversion is easily seen, just as the connection of Lazarus' coming forth with Jesus' voice. When once the dead man was made alive, his coming out of the tomb was but the natural response to the Saviour's call; and so if there be spiritual life, it is the most natural thing in the world, that the gracious invitations of God's word should call forth faith and repentance. But how the loud voice of Jesus was accompanied with the restoration of life to the dead man, so that his ear heard it and his limbs obeyed it, who can explain, save that Jesus' prayer was equivalent to the prophet's invocation, "Come from the four winds, O breath, and breathe upon these slain that they may live"? (Ezek. xxxvii. 9). So in addressing the spiritually dead the wisdom of God is able to say, "Turn ye at my reproof: Behold, I will pour out my spirit unto you; I will make known my words unto you" (Prov. i. 23).

Hence we see why conversion may be repeated, while regeneration is never so spoken of, but as a change effected once for all. Eternal life can only be once communicated; but the activity of life may be renewed and called forth again and again, as often as it has fallen into sloth. The call may need to be addressed to a real Christian who has become careless, "Awake, thou that sleepest, and arise from the dead, and Christ shall shine upon thee" (Eph. v. 14). There is life presupposed here, it is a sleeper in a field of the dead, where "thousands have sunk on the ground overpowered, the weary to sleep, and the wounded to die." If he be not awakened, and his eyes enlightened, he may sleep the sleep of death; but he is called to awake and arise from among the dead. So a disciple of Christ may need to be called to repent and do the first works. So Peter, after his denial of his Lord, needed to be converted, but not to be born again; for Jesus prayed for him that his faith fail not (Luke xxii. 32). That faith which had been given him not by flesh and blood but by the Father in heaven (Matt. xvi. 17), which enabled him to cleave to Jesus when many turned back (John vi. 68), also made his heart melt at the look of Jesus (Luke xxii. 61), and brought him back to the Saviour in penitent love, when Judas turned away in despair.

We find also that the necessity of regeneration is asserted in far more absolute terms than that of conversion. "Except a man be born anew, he cannot see the kingdom of God." "Except a man be born of water and the Spirit, he cannot enter the kingdom of God. Ye must be born again" (John iii. 3, 5, 7); "If any man be in Christ, he is a new creature" (2 Cor. v. 17); "If ye know that He is righteous, ye know that every one that doeth righteousness is begotten of Him" (1 John ii. 29). These statements are unlimited, applying to all, every, any man. There is no such absolute statement of the necessity of conversion. Jesus indeed says, addressing men who showed evidence of sin and selfishness, "Except ye turn and become as little children, ye shall in nowise enter the kingdom of heaven" (Matt. xviii. 3); and the prophet cries to his ungodly people, "Turn ye, turn ye, why will ye die?" (Ezek. xxxiii. 11); but all such sayings have reference to those to whom they are addressed, and do not necessarily imply that every one of mankind must pass through a conscious process of conversion. On the contrary, it was prophesied of John the Baptist, "he shall be filled with the Holy Spirit even from his mother's womb;" and his spiritual growth is described as unmarked by any decisive change; "the child grew and waxed strong in spirit, and was in the desert until the day of his showing unto Israel" (Luke i. 15, 80). To be filled with the Holy Spirit can hardly denote anything less than regeneration; and thus it seems to be taught that this vital change may take place even in infancy. This is confirmed by Jesus' saying of little children, "Of such is the kingdom of God" (Mark x. 14 and parallels),[1] when that is taken along with His statement that except one be born of water and the Spirit he cannot enter the kingdom of God. If regeneration be a creative act of divine power on the soul, the occurrence of it in infancy implies no contradiction, but only the same mystery as is involved in the communication to infants of mental and moral capacities and powers that are afterwards brought forth into actual exercise; whereas conversion, faith, and repentance cannot be ascribed to infants without doing violence to psychological truth. The history and experience of many who have been brought up under Christian influences confirm this; for in such cases there is often no decisive change, such as conversion commonly is; though there is real evidence of a God-ward

---

[1] Some good interpreters indeed understand "such" to mean men of a childlike spirit; but it is more accordant with the general use of the word and the scope of the context, to understand it of actual children. When it is said the kingdom is of such, the meaning is not necessarily that these are all its members, but only that it includes these; as when Jesus says of those persecuted for righteousness' sake, "theirs is the kingdom of heaven" (Matt. v. 10).

and heaven-ward principle striving against the natural, selfish, and earthly tendencies of the soul.

In the case of those who are born again in mature life, regeneration and conversion coincide in point of time; for the new spiritual life is essentially active, and where its exercise is not delayed by the imperfect development of the mental powers, shows itself at once in turning to God in Christ in obedience to the gospel call. Hence, while the soul is said by theologians to be passive in regeneration, according to the passive forms of expression used in Scripture, that means simply that it is acted upon in a mysterious way by the power of the Holy Spirit. But the soul is never absolutely inactive, and within our consciousness there is always activity in one direction or another, for sin, or for God. There may often be a hesitation and halting for a time between two opinions; but when the decisive choice is made, we cannot but believe that there has been an influence secretly at work beyond and beneath consciousness; though within the range of consciousness there has been no cessation of activity, but only a change of activity. Strong language has sometimes been used, comparing the natural heart of man to a stock or stone, and Scripture speaks of hearts of stone; but this language is rhetorical and not exact; and those who have used it admit that the soul is never absolutely like a stock or stone, nay it is worse than if it were merely inert, for naturally it actively resists the gospel.

The result to which this secret work of the Holy Spirit leads, and in which it shows its reality, is variously described in Scripture as coming to Christ, believing in Christ, turning to God, repentance towards God, believing in God through Christ. Christ is ever presented in the New Testament as the revealer and representative of God to us, so that the exercise of soul by which we are brought into a right religious state is sometimes viewed as having God, and sometimes Christ for its object; but we are always to understand that in reality it is directed to both, through Christ to God. If Jesus asks us to believe in him, it is because He doeth the works of God, and the Father is in Him and He in the Father; if He calls us to repent and turn from sin to God, it is because the kingdom of God is at hand in virtue of His appearing.

The two exercises of faith and repentance are not separate things, of which one may take place without the other, or one at one time and the other at another; they are inseparably connected as acts of the soul's conversion or reconciliation to God; though for certain purposes they need to be distinguished and considered separately. Together they give a complete view of the great change by which a man from being an enemy to God, as he is by nature, comes to be at peace with Him as his God and Father. In one aspect of it that is a change of character and conduct, from the practice of sin to that of holiness, and this is what is called repentance, *i.e.* a change of mind. This has relation more especially to God, as the lawgiver and moral judge of all the earth; and implies a sense of the evil of sin in His sight, and a turning from it. But this would not be possible, unless we were assured that God, though holy, is also merciful, and ready to receive sinners to His fellowship, and grant them forgiveness and favour. This assurance we have in the gospel, which declares that God pardons sinners for Christ's sake; and therefore our coming to Him must be in reliance on Christ as our Mediator, or on God through Christ. This is what is meant by faith in the New Testament, where it is spoken of as the means of our salvation. It is not, as has too often been thought, the belief of a doctrine or set of doctrines, however true and important these may be, nor the acceptance of a new view about God, and His relation to man, and His love and purposes for man; but a childlike trust in God and Christ. No doubt Jesus and His apostles did call upon men to believe the gospel which they proclaimed, and that implied in many cases the acceptance of truths that had not been known before, and sometimes the giving up false theories and even whole systems of belief. But they called for much more than that: they called on men to have trust or confidence in God as gracious, merciful, and loving, and in Jesus as the Son of God who had come to save the world by His death; and they never speak of any one being saved by faith where there is not such personal trust in God and Christ. So it was in the case of the centurion of Capernaum (Matt. viii. 5–11); of the harlot in Simon's house (Luke vii. 44–50); of the palsied man and his friends (Mark ii. 5, 6), and others who believed during our Lord's earthly ministry: so too in the case of those who were converted on the day of Pentecost and afterwards by the preaching of the disciples of Jesus. The amount of knowledge that these various converts possessed, and the doctrines that they believed, must have been very different in different cases, sometimes more and sometimes less; what was common to them all was their trust in Christ as revealing the grace and love of God, and through Him in God. This trust in God we can also see is the same as that which is so often expressed in the Old Testament, especially in the Psalms, as the essence of Israel's religion; and the only difference is that in the New Testament God is revealed as in Christ reconciling the world to Himself, not imputing their trespasses to them; whereas in earlier times all that was distinctly revealed was, that God is merciful and gracious, and that there is forgiveness with Him.

Since God is revealed by Christ, not only as merciful and gracious, but also as holy, and hating sin with a perfect hatred, even while He loves and forgives sinners; and since Jesus' work was to save His people from their sins; that trust in God that responds to this gospel must be accompanied with a desire, or at least a willingness, to be delivered from sin; and that implies a real sorrow and hatred of sin, a confession of it to God, and a desire and effort after the holiness that He loves and requires. This is what is denoted by repentance in the New Testament; where it means, not merely regret for a past act of wrong, but a change of mind. It is most simply and beautifully depicted by our Lord in the parable of the prodigal son (Luke xv. 11–32), from which we may learn the most essential points about it. We see there that it implies an entire change of life and conduct, as well as a frank confession of sin. The undutiful son returns from the far country, where he had spent his substance in riotous living, and desires henceforth to live with and obey his father, while he frankly confesses his sin and unworthiness, and attempts no excuse for his conduct. But the change is much deeper than the outward conduct; he has now evidently a quite different state of feeling towards his father from that which he had before. Hence it is said of him at the turning-point of his career, " he came to himself," as if he had been beside himself, or out of his right mind before. This change, too, is connected with faith; for it was the feeling of trust in his father's love and kindness that encouraged him to return, otherwise a conviction of sin might only have driven him to despair. Such was its effect on Judas, even when it moved him to confess and forsake his sin; but while Jesus spoke of the evil of sin, and warned men of its terrible consequences, He at the same time encouraged them to trust in God's mercy, and it was the very purpose of this parable to exhibit that mercy.

We can see therefore how that coming to God through Christ, which implies both faith and repentance, is really a decisive moral change in the soul; and how it may truly be said, that the sinner who repents, " was dead and is alive again, and was lost and is found." The faith by which we are saved is thus no mere intellectual act or head work; it implies the consent of the heart, as well as the assent of the mind, to the saving work of Christ; and cannot be conceived as remaining a mere unpractical belief in the soul, but must be active in the way of repentance, love, and holiness. This is the sort of faith of which Paul makes so much; of which he says, not only that we are justified by it, without works of law; but that it unites us to Christ, makes us children of God, and works by love. This great change, which is a matter of real experience in the case of multitudes, is ever ascribed in Scripture, not to any effort, or industry, or goodness of men, but to God, calling us by His grace in the gospel, and also by the power of His Spirit working secretly in our hearts, inclining and enabling us to comply with the call. This makes us new creatures, animated by a new principle or motive, which is faith working by love, or love as the effect of faith. This constitutes as great a difference among men morally as the presence of animal life does between the living and the lifeless in the physical world. This seems to be implied in the scriptural representations of the saving change as a new life, being begotten of God, a new creation, being raised from the dead, and the like. These are too numerous and uniform to be explained as mere figures of speech, though clearly they are not to be taken literally, but as indicating a true analogy. Just as animated matter is moved not only by mechanical laws but by those of life; and just as rational creatures are guided not merely by laws of animal life and instinct, but by those of reason and conscience; so those who are turned to God in Christ are animated by a principle of divine love, to which unconverted men are strangers.

This may to a certain extent be verified by observation, not indeed in individual cases, the discrimination of which eludes our scrutiny, but in general, wherever the distinction between Christians and non-Christians can be seen on a large scale. The entire absence of love to God in the Christian sense implies a state which may be as truly described as being destitute of spiritual life as a crystal is destitute of animal life, or a dog is destitute of intellectual life. There is indeed this difference, that such a state in man is an abnormal and degraded state, and so also one from which he may and should be raised; and therefore, especially since it implies the possession of intellectual as well as animal life, it may also be considered as a state of disease, as it is sometimes called in Scripture. But that it implies as great a difference as that which separates the living from the lifeless in the lower kingdoms of nature, may be seen by considering the moral character of the motives that must animate those destitute of love to God. These may be various, and must be judged each for itself, as love of self, or of earthly things, natural affection, friendship, patriotism, or philanthropy. They may be divided in general into those that are selfish, and those that are unselfish yet ungodly.

As to the former there is little difficulty. There are and have always been men who have no higher motive than selfishness, and no higher aim than self-interest in some form or other more or less refined. Of all such we need have no hesitation in saying that they are destitute of what is really a higher kind of life, the life of godliness, such a life as Jesus lived. Whether their ruling passion be love of pleasure, or of wealth, or of power, or of honour; and in whatever way it may be pursued, whether so as to lead to unbridled indulgence of appetite and passion, or to a hypocritical pretence of virtue, or to a really sober, honest, and industrious life ; still if it is only self that is had in view in all this, there is a part of human nature that is utterly insensible and inactive in such men ; and as to it they are really dead. Some philosophers have attempted to explain human nature on the assumption that there are no principles or motives in it which are not at bottom self-regarding; and there have been many men of the world who have acted on this principle, holding that every man has his price, and that there is no such thing as disinterested virtue. But the policy of such worldlings has ever been defeated by Christian principle, and the philosophy that underlies it is shallow and onesided.

It is more difficult to judge of lives animated by motives that are not selfish, and yet not distinctly Christian or even religious. Such are the family affections, friendship, patriotism, philanthropy. The family affections may indeed be merely instinctive, and in some cases may even be selfish, when a man loves his family as a part of himself, or for his own gratification and pride ; but they may be, and often are, in the highest degree unselfish. Still more does the love of friends, of one's country, or of men as such, possess a disinterested character, and raise those who are ruled by such motives to a higher life than that of the mere selfish worldling. Yet these unselfish motives may, no less than the selfish ones, prompt to acts of falsehood, wrong, or cruelty, when they are not combined with a regard for righteousness and morality. Such was the case with some of the best of the ancient Greeks and Romans, whose patriotism, though sincere and disinterested, was unscrupulous, and not ruled by any high principle. In such cases, must we not say, that the want of regard to right for its own sake shows that, though not dead to the sympathetic feelings, they have their moral nature destroyed or undeveloped, and so have no life in fellowship with God, who is revealed in the moral sense of man, even more directly than in the phenomena of nature?

When, however, unselfish motives are accompanied with regard for truth and right, and men are found seeking to live for their families, their friends, their country, or their fellow-men, in accordance with virtue, or when they have been making virtue itself their great aim, even though they have no clear knowledge of the living and true God, and no conscious love to Him, we cannot say that such are destitute of spiritual life; but should rather say that they really are living to God, though they know it not, if they are indeed living for that moral goodness which is the essential character of God. For in so far as they regard and pursue true virtue, they are seeking that which is the will and the nature of God, whether they know it or not. Such cases there may have been among the heathen, and we know of Socrates and Epictetus; but history shows them to be very rare apart from Christianity, for it is hard to attain to a real love of moral goodness in all its extent, except through the revelation of it in the character of God in Jesus Christ.

The Bible view is, that the love of God is the love of goodness; to seek God is to seek goodness (Ps. xcvii. 10; Amos v. 4-15; Zeph. ii. 3; Isa. lv. 6, 7; 1 John v. 3): and so we can understand how the knowledge and love of God is eternal life; and they who have it are born of God (John xvii. 3; 1 John ii. 29, iv. 7, 8). One who is destitute of regard for moral goodness, however he may be endowed with prudence, benevolence, or patriotism, is as to one all-important part of his nature, practically dead. It may, however, be said that the love of goodness does not necessarily imply the love of God, and that there may be a want of love to God, where there is not that moral and spiritual death, which is involved in the want of love to goodness: and examples may be found in Buddha, and in some of the modern agnostic or atheistic philosophers, who have a high sense and regard for moral excellence, to show that ignorance or denial of God does not necessarily imply the absence of the highest life of the soul. But to this it may be replied, that when sincere lovers of goodness have denied or ignored a personal God, this has been due to an extreme reaction against an immoral heathen mythology, as in the case of Buddha and some Greek philosophers, or to some distorted view of the phenomena of the universe, by which men have been hindered from seeing them to be the work of a perfectly good Being. But if there really is such a Being, then the love of goodness is the love of His character, even in those who unhappily may not be able to believe His existence. Thus Paul, while he describes the heathen as alienated from the life of God because of the ignorance that is in them (Eph. iv. 18), yet recognises those who built an altar to an unknown God as worshipping unknowing the true God (Acts xvii. 23); and those who do the things of the law of God as showing the work of the law written in their hearts (Rom. ii. 14, 15).

We are not therefore entitled to deny, that there may be real spiritual life outside the pale of those who have received the revelation of God's grace, and in men who know not the living God. The occurrence of some such cases illustrates the power and sovereignty of the Spirit of God, who can, where it seems good to Him, change men's hearts even without the ordinary means. But it is a simple historical fact, that nowhere have purity, love, and truth been generally loved and diffused in any community, except where the doctrines of Christianity have been preached. Only there has the Spirit of God been poured out on all flesh, because the actual knowledge of God, as revealed in Christ crucified, is the only thing that can bring home to the mass of men the love of God, which is the moving spring of the new life. But the Spirit of God did work on many under the Old Testament, and doubtless on many also in heathendom, though these were but scattered lights, and could effect no general reformation.

CHAPTER VI.

THE WORK OF THE SPIRIT UNITING US TO CHRIST.

THE regenerating work of the Holy Spirit, producing faith and repentance, effects a union of believers to Christ and to one another in Christ, a union which, though inward and unseen, is yet most real in itself and powerful in its results. Our very faith in Christ of itself implies the union of a covenant of love and friendship : for it is a mutual interchange of promises and assurances of fidelity. There is on the part of Christ the offer of His grace and help in the gospel ; and our faith responds to that by a trusting acceptance of the offer. Then there is on our part the giving of ourselves to Christ to be led and saved by Him, and His acceptance of us as His people, and assurance that He will save us. These reciprocal offers and acceptances constitute a covenant, and effect a union of alliance and affection between Christ and believers. So it is often represented in Scripture ; as when He says, " My sheep hear my voice, and I know them, and they follow me: and I give unto them eternal life" (John x. 27, 28). By their mutual recognition and acceptance of each other as Leader and followers, the union between the Shepherd and His sheep is formed. So too when the relation between Christ and His Church is compared to the marriage union of husband and wife, one point of the comparison is, that it is formed by mutual consent and the interchange of vows of faithful love (2 Cor. xi. 2, 3 ; Eph. v. 22–33 ; John iii. 29).

But since Christian faith and repentance are the result of the working of the Spirit of God in our hearts, and the same Spirit also wrought in Christ as the incarnate Son of God in His work on earth, the union of believers to Christ is something more and deeper than a mere covenant union of mutual trust, love, and sympathy. Beneath the agreement in these feelings, there is the one Spirit of God that is the source of them, working alike in Christ and in His people, and making them spiritually one body, because all animated by one Spirit. This is the other favourite illustration of Paul. The Church, he says, is the body of Christ; He is the Head and every believer is a member of the body, each having its own proper function, but all united to each other and to their common Head (Rom. xii. 4, 5; 1 Cor. xii. 12-31; Eph. i. 22, 23, iv. 4-16). That which makes them thus one is the one Spirit dwelling in them all; and the indwelling of the Spirit is the same thing as the indwelling of Christ, whose Spirit He is (Eph. iii. 16, 17). The one life which animates all believers is the life of Christ; and so it is truly said Christ lives in them, and is their life (Gal. ii. 20; Col. iii. 3, 4). Those in whom Christ is by His Spirit are also described as being in Christ (Rom. viii. 1, 9, 10). The same twofold and seemingly opposite way of speaking is used by Jesus, when He illustrates His disciples' relation to Him by the parable of the vine and its branches (John xv. 1-8). They are in Him, but also He is in them: and both statements are needed fully to express the union from different points of view. Looked at extensively, as it were, believers are in Christ, as the branches are in the vine, being parts of the one whole, making up the full complement of the plant as an extended organism, consisting of root, stem, and branches. But looked at intensively, so to say, it is equally true, that the vine is in the branches: the life of the vine is in them, the sap of the vine flows through them and nourishes them; the fruit of the vine is borne by them. So believers are in Christ, because belonging to Him as His covenant people, and they abide in Him by faith; while He is in them by His Holy Spirit dwelling and working in them.

The reality of this is shown by the life and character of Christ appearing in them, especially in the emotions of godliness, brotherly kindness, and charity, that animated Him, and also animate them. This threefold form of love, to God our Father in heaven, to the children of God as our brethren in Christ, and to all men as those whom God loves and for whom He gave His Son, is the characteristic mark of Christians, and the common sentiment of the Christian Church. It necessarily flows from faith in Jesus Christ and conversion to God, wherever these are genuine; and it constitutes the actual and working unity of the Church of Christ. This is what is meant by the unity of the Spirit, which Paul exhorts Christians to give diligence to keep (Eph. iv. 3); and probably also by "the love of the Spirit,"[1] to which he appeals as a motive for united prayer (Rom. xv. 30). In virtue of this unity, earnest Christians, however unlike and even opposed they may be in nationality, character, customs, and opinions on many points, find themselves at one in their common faith and love of their Saviour and interest in His cause: they have an affection and concern for one another for the sake of their common Lord, and have similar sentiments and desires for the wellbeing of their fellow-men. This unity of the Spirit requires indeed to be cultivated; for it may be hindered or interrupted by the selfish feelings, or narrow prejudices, or worldly sentiments that are apt to linger in the hearts even of those who ought to be brethren. If any one is unwilling to humble or deny himself for the sake of his Master and his brethren; or is making the interests of his nation, or his order, or his party, of more importance than those of the cause of Christ and the world's salvation; or has too narrow ideas of the kingdom and work of Christ, and considers the opinions, or customs, or forms of his own section of the Church essential to Christianity; such an one will not find himself drawn in sympathy and love to

[1] This phrase might also mean the love that the Holy Spirit has to us, and as Paul elsewhere speaks of the mind and the will of the Spirit, he might quite well have ascribed love also to Him. But as he never uses any expression exactly similar, it is perhaps more likely that it means the love of Christians which is wrought in them by the agency of the Holy Spirit.

all who love the Lord Jesus, but repelled and shut out from some of them : and in so far as any of these tendencies prevail, the unity of the Spirit is marred and weakened. Hence we need to give diligence to keep it. We do so just by following the leading and yielding to the movements of the Holy Spirit, or, to express the same thing in other words, by living the life of faith and love that is implanted in us by the Spirit's work of regeneration.

It is not an adequate expression of what the New Testament teaches to say, as Schleiermacher did, that the Holy Spirit is just the common life that animates the body of Christians. That is the result of the Spirit's work; but we must go beyond the effect to the cause that produces it, to find the Holy Spirit Himself. Yet undoubtedly the Christian spirit or frame of mind, as a humble, devout, unselfish, holy, and loving disposition, which unites those who have it in common devotion to God and Christ, and a common longing and effort for the deliverance of man from sin and misery, is the chief manifestation of the existence and activity of a divine Agent in the hearts of men.

This aspect of the work of the Holy Spirit affords the basis of the doctrine of the Catholic Church of Christ, as unfolded in Paul's later epistles, in its ideal as invisible, and in its approximate realizations by means of the various gifts, offices, and functions of its members, according to the order and directions given by Christ and His apostles. The consideration of what that order and these directions are, belongs to the department of Church government :[1] the work of the Spirit, which secures the real inward growth and perfection of the Church, is wrought in its members individually, each for himself, by the process of sanctification, edification, and comfort.

[1] On these subjects the reader is referred to previous handbooks in this series: *The Church*, by William Binnie, D.D., Professor of Church History, Aberdeen; and *Presbyterianism*, by the Rev. John M'Pherson, M.A., Findhorn.

CHAPTER VII.

THE WORK OF THE SPIRIT IN SANCTIFICATION.

IN conversion, as we have seen, according to Scripture and Christian experience, the Holy Spirit effects a radical change in the soul. By working in us faith and repentance, He imparts to us a new principle of life, the principle of godliness or love to God, which is the ruling motive of every genuine Christian. This seems to be what is called in one remarkable passage "the seed of God" (1 John iii. 9), and in another "that which is begotten of the Spirit" (John iii. 6); and the possession of this divine principle of life makes an essential difference between those who are born again and even the best of those animated by merely selfish or earthly motives. But this does not imply that the child of God is at once perfect in holiness. On the contrary, since the Spirit of God may and often does lay hold of the very lowest and most sinful; the materials, so to speak, on which this work is wrought are often very unlikely; and as it is not done magically, or by mere power, but by the influence of grace, in accordance with the essential constitution of man, and in the way of a vital process, it is only by degrees that the soul is completely renewed. A new principle or ruling motive is imparted by regeneration, and the Christian is no longer under the influence of selfishness as his highest impulse, but is really possessed with love to God and faith in Jesus Christ. This new principle more or less influences the whole nature: the thoughts, the feelings, the desires, the actions, all are affected by it: so that in a true sense it may be said there is an entire renewal. The regenerate has not only a new belief, or a new hope, or a new love, or a new conduct, but all these together; he is a new man, a new creature.

Yet his renewal is not complete in any part. The faith of the Christian, though real and sincere, is not perfect at first, but often mingled and interrupted with distrust; his love, though genuine, may not be strong enough to encounter hardships or temptations: in a word, though he has a germ of spiritual life implanted within him, which in principle is higher than anything of which unrenewed men partake, he is still beset with allurements to sin, and possessed with tendencies or habits of yielding to these allurements. He really loves God and hates sin; that is the ruling principle of his soul: but that does not remove all possibility of sin, it does not make the pleasures of sin less attractive to his senses, or the self-denial that God requires less painful to flesh and blood: it does not destroy the power of habit which may have been contracted by former acts of self-indulgence; nor does it obviate the possibility of missing the path of duty through mistake or heedlessness. Such is the state in which the New Testament describes the converts to Christianity as being, with their hearts filled with a new affection, love to God and Christ, yet prone to many sins, sometimes of a gross and shocking nature, and needing to have the most plain moral duties enforced on them. The spirit is willing, but the flesh is weak; nay, the flesh lusteth against the spirit.

By these adverse influences the principle of love to God in the heart might be overcome and choked, were it not continually nourished and strengthened by the same power that implanted it at first. If the influence of the Holy Spirit in regeneration were a merely transient impulse, however powerful, the renewal effected by it would not be complete, and might not be lasting. The new impulse of love to God would be continually opposed by the remaining tendencies and temptations to evil, and would be in danger of either degenerating into a mere sentiment, without influence on practical life, or being entirely extinguished in course of time. In order to escape these dangers, the new life in the soul must be fed and encouraged, so that it may grow and gain strength; and this, Scripture declares, is done by the Holy Spirit in the work of progressive renewal or sanctification.

The Holy Spirit is said not only to be given, but to dwell in Christians (Rom. viii. 9, 11; 1 Cor. vi. 19; John xiv. 17; 1 John ii. 27); and this indicates His continual working. As the Spirit of God is in His essence omnipresent, His coming upon any one denotes, not any local movement, but His beginning to work upon such a one in a way He had not done before; and so His abiding upon, or dwelling in men, means His continuing to influence them as He had begun. The Holy Spirit kindled the new life of faith and love in a twofold way, outwardly by presenting the grace and love of God in the gospel, and inwardly by opening the heart to receive that grace and love. In a like twofold manner He continues His work, and thereby nurtures the faith that He implanted at first. By the Holy Spirit the grace of God as revealed in Christ continues to be presented to the soul; and the gospel, as it is the means of our new birth, so also is it the means of our growth in spiritual life. Hence Peter, after reminding Christians that they have been born again of incorruptible seed through the Word of God, exhorts them as new-born babes to "long for the spiritual milk which is without guile,[1] that they may grow thereby unto salvation" (1 Pet. ii. 2). The spiritual nourishment of our souls is the gospel, or Christ who is presented in the gospel. Christ crucified is, as Augustine said, both milk for babes and meat for men. This spiritual food nourishes the soul as it is received by faith and love; and the gospel presenting Christ to us calls forth these graces into continual and active exercise, and so promotes their growth and the increasing perfection of the Christian character. The revelation

---

[1] This rendering of the Revised Version is more in accordance with the usage of the language than "the sincere milk of the word;" but though the reference to ch. i. 23 is thereby effaced, we need not doubt that it is the word of God that is meant.

of God that is made in the person, and teaching, and work of Jesus, and in the blessings that flow from these, is most fitted to increase and confirm that faith or trustful reliance on God's mercy, and that repentance or aversion from evil and turning to God, which form the beginning and principle of Christian life. These when continued in exercise tend to promote that life, by acquiring the strength and persistency of a habit, and gradually weakening or expelling contrary habits and overcoming temptations. This is that walking by the Spirit (Gal. v. 25), after the Spirit (Rom. viii. 4–14), in Christ (Col. ii. 6), repeatedly enjoined on Christians as the work of their life and the means of their growth. It denotes a continual exercise of faith and repentance as at the first, looking ever to Christ and to God, with the same feelings of trust, penitence, and love, as when the gospel first came to the soul with its blessed message of glad tidings. For this end the Word of God must be the constant study of the believer; and it is a means that the Holy Spirit uses for his sanctification.

But the Spirit also acts more directly on the soul in this work. The various virtues of the Christian character are described as the fruit of the Spirit (Gal. v. 22); by the Spirit God reveals to us His hidden wisdom (1 Cor. ii. 10); by the Spirit we are transformed into the image of the Lord (2 Cor. iii. 18); by the Spirit we mortify the deeds of the body (Rom. viii. 13); by the Spirit we are strengthened in faith and love (Eph. iii. 16). These and other passages indicate a work of the Spirit that consists not merely in presenting to us the revelation of God in Christ, which is fitted to draw our faith and love into continual exercise; but in opening our minds to perceive and our hearts to feel the grace of God thus revealed, and so actually producing in us the exercise of faith and love. We find from experience, that in the progress as in the beginning of Christian life, we are not entirely dependent on the external presentation of God's grace. The very same passages of God's Word or views of its truths, that at one time produced the most deep and salutary effects, enlightening the mind, melting the heart to penitence and love, stimulating and encouraging the soul to resolutions and efforts after holiness, may at another time be read or heard, and understood exactly in the same way, and yet fail to make any such impression These spiritual effects, that are not traceable merely to the mora influence of the truth, and that can as little be accounted for by our own will or by external circumstances, are most reasonably to be ascribed to that direct working of the Holy Spirit on the souls of believers of which Scripture speaks. If in the primitive Church the Spirit of God was recognised as the author of the extraordinary gifts of prophecy, tongues, healing: must we not assign to the same source that spiritual insight by which the truths of God are opened up, that devotional fervour that finds spontaneous utterance in earnest pleading prayer, and that zeal for good works that effects things for the good of men that seemed impossible before? The abiding graces, of faith, hope, and love, are in Paul's estimate higher and more divine than the best of the supernatural gifts, and they cannot be conceived as less directly due to the agency of the Holy Spirit.

More particularly, the Holy Spirit works in the process of sanctification by producing in the soul those special virtues which may be lacking in particular persons, or needed on particular occasions. One Christian, for example, may be constitutionally defective in courage, another in meekness, another in patience, and so on. These special qualities the Spirit of God can and does bestow; as Paul reminds Timothy, who seems to have been naturally of a timid and shrinking disposition, " God gave us not a spirit of fearfulness, but of power, and of love, and of discipline" (2 Tim. i. 7); or as the fiery spirit of the son of thunder was chastened and refined, so that he became the Apostle of love. There are special aspects of God's revelation in Christ fitted to draw forth special virtues, and to discourage and check the faults opposed to them ; and these the Holy Spirit uses for these ends ; as we may see how Paul's second letter to Timothy sets forth those views of Christian truth and experience that are most likely to encourage and strengthen a timid disciple; and Jesus, when He had occasion to rebuke the intolerant zeal of James and John, showed them in word and deed the grace and love of His mission.[1] The dealings of Providence too, more especially the trials and afflictions of life, are made the means of promoting and perfecting in believers special virtues in which they may be defective, such as meekness, patience, hope. At the same time, there is also a direct agency of the Holy Spirit here; for all these virtues are described as the fruit of the Spirit; they are all developments in various directions of the right state of heart towards God, expressed in faith and repentance, which is wrought and maintained by the Spirit of God in the heart. The new life of Christianity is a unity; and though, on account of the imperfect and abnormal condition of most Christians, it does not show itself with perfect symmetry; yet it tends towards moral excellence and perfection in every direction, and the more vigorous the central principle of religious life is, the more will particular virtues be developed and increased.

The Spirit's work of sanctification is thus the continuance and development of regeneration; and is related to it as preservation is to creation in the natural world. But just as preservation differs from creation in this, that in it God works by means, and with the co-operation of the creatures; so in the Spirit's work of sanctification there is a co-operation of the human will, such as cannot be admitted in regeneration. In implanting the new life at first, the Holy Spirit has to deal with a soul, that is indeed essentially active, but in regard to spiritual religion insensible or opposed to the call of God. Hence this work is entirely due

---

[1] Luke ix. 54–56. The words, "Ye know not what manner of spirit ye are of: for the Son of man came not to destroy men's lives, but to save them," are indeed of doubtful authenticity; but they are thoroughly in the Spirit of Christ, and more likely to have been omitted than added in the time of the oldest MSS. Anyhow we may be sure that it was what he saw and felt of the love of Christ, that softened the natural character of John.

to the divine power ; we are His workmanship, created in Christ Jesus unto good works. But in the preservation and development of the new life, the Spirit has to deal with a soul that is now spiritually alive, that is able and inclined to work in the same direction as His work. Hence in this process of sanctification we are called to be fellow-workers with God ; we are to work out our own salvation with fear and trembling, because it is God that worketh in us to will and to do. Such exhortations continually occur in the Epistles, in close connection with statements of the work of God by His Spirit in our sanctification. The knowledge we have of the reality of that work ought not to lead us to be less earnest and diligent in our own efforts, but rather more so: for it assures us that our efforts shall not be in vain, as we might fear they would be, if we had only them to look to for success. Nor does the sanctifying work of the Holy Spirit render our co-operation needless ; for though the Spirit's power is indeed divine, and therefore all-sufficient, yet it is exercised in a way suited to our nature, not only as men, but as now having spiritual life, and able to know, desire, and seek for spiritual blessings. The fear and trembling, with which Paul says Christians ought to engage in the work, are not due to uncertainty or want of hope as to the issue, but are the emotions that ought naturally to arise from the knowledge that we are so closely associated with God in the work. If we have any right apprehension of the greatness, the glory, the holiness of God, we must feel that it is a solemn and awful thing to be fellow-workers with the high and lofty One who inhabiteth eternity, whose name is holy. With what reverence should we engage in the work of purifying ourselves, how careful should we be that our hearts are right with God, and our ends and aims in harmony with His, how fearful lest by heedlessness or self-seeking we provoke His holy anger ! In Scripture there are warnings not only to unbelievers that they resist not the Holy Spirit, but also to Christians that they do not grieve that blessed Agent (Eph. iv. 30) ; and it is indicated that the Spirit is grieved when we indulge in anger, bitterness, or malice, or anything opposed to God's holy law. If we rebel and grieve His Holy Spirit, God may turn to be our enemy and fight against us (Isa. lxiii. 10); and whenever we fall into any grievous sin, we have reason to pray with the Psalmist, "Take not thy holy spirit from me" (Ps. li. 11). If it is the holy God who thus works in us by His Spirit, well may we be filled with fear and trembling as we work out our own salvation.

Yet we have the assurance that God our Saviour is able to keep us from falling, and to present us blameless before the presence of His glory with exceeding joy (Jude 24); that saints are kept by the power of God through faith unto salvation (1 Pet. i. 5); and that He who hath begun a good work in us will perfect it until the day of Christ (Phil. i. 6). So we may give ourselves to this work in the confidence and hope that such promises are fitted to inspire, and be strong in the Lord who sanctifies us, and who has said, "I will never leave thee nor forsake thee."

CHAPTER VIII.

THE WORK OF THE SPIRIT AS A WITNESS AND TEACHER.

THE agency of the Holy Spirit in originating and carrying on the new life of Christian faith and love in the soul may be said to include the whole of what He does in us for our salvation; for it includes the renewal and sanctification of the whole man, and might be traced in detail through the various parts of our nature, the mind, the conscience, the heart, the will. To attempt this, however, would involve us in psychological discussions on which Scripture, as it is written for practical rather than theoretical ends, affords little direct light. There is, however, one special aspect of the Spirit's work which it is practically important to consider separately, and which has a distinct prominence given it in the New Testament, His work on the mind, as a witness and teacher. It was in this character especially that Jesus promised the Holy Spirit to His disciples (John xiv. 26, xv. 26); in the character of a witness He is appealed to by the apostles (Acts v. 32; Heb. ii. 4); and His work in teaching and witnessing is described as assuring the faith of believers (Rom. viii. 16; 1 Cor. ii. 4, 10–16; 1 John ii. 20, 27, v. 7–11). These and other passages speak so emphatically of a witness or teaching of the Spirit, as to lead us to inquire specially what this means, and how it is realized. They describe the Spirit of God as not merely working in us, but addressing Himself to us, and communicating knowledge and certainty of the truth.

According to the usage of Scripture language, the words,

"teach," "testify," and the like, may be used of impersonal things which by their existence or appearance convey knowledge to men. So it is said, "The heavens declare the glory of God, and the firmament showeth his handiwork. Day unto day uttereth speech, and night unto night teacheth knowledge" (Ps. xix. 1); and again, the water and the blood bear witness as well as the Spirit (1 John v. 8). In some of the passages above referred to, the Holy Spirit may be said to testify simply in this way, the fact of Jesus' disciples being endowed with spiritual gifts being a proof of the divine authority and exaltation of Jesus. But it is impossible fairly to apply this explanation to all those statements; some of them plainly have a different meaning. Where passages from the Old Testament are quoted with the phrase, "the Holy Spirit saith," "the Holy Spirit beareth witness" (Heb. iii. 7, x. 15), the meaning is that the sacred writers having been moved by the Holy Spirit, their teaching is that of the Spirit to us. In the same sense Paul speaks of the Holy Spirit testifying, through the utterances of Christian prophets, that bonds and afflictions awaited him (Acts xx. 23). Now when we find such expressions used; we cannot doubt that Jesus' saying to His disciples, that the Holy Spirit would teach them, and testify along with them (John xv. 26, xvi. 13–15), meant that He would communicate truth to them, and through them to others. This promise includes the inspiration of the apostles and prophets of the New Testament; while in the light of other sayings we can hardly doubt that it conveys also a promise of the teaching of the Spirit to all who believe in Jesus. For John says to Christians in general, "Ye have an anointing from the Holy One, and ye know all things, . . . and his anointing teacheth you concerning all things" (1 John ii. 20, 27). This plainly means that this divine anointing, which is the Holy Spirit, teaches us not merely by the fact of the effects which it produces, or by the utterances of inspired men, but by a direct communication to our souls. The same thing is taught by Paul, when he says that "his speech and his preaching were in demonstration of the Spirit and of power," that is, his gospel had been proved to them by the Spirit and by power. This cannot refer to any miraculous gifts of the Spirit; for these would have formed a sign, such as the Jews vainly sought: it can only mean, that the Holy Spirit showed to the hearers the truth of the gospel. So also, when he writes to the Thessalonians, that the gospel came to them in power, and in the Holy Spirit, and in much assurance (1 Thess. i. 5), he must mean that the Holy Spirit enabled them to see the gospel to be the word of God, and to embrace it as such. This is in the fullest sense a testimony of the Spirit; because the gospel comes to us as the word of God given by His Spirit, and the same Spirit enables us to see that it is so. This latter work is not an objective communication of truth additional to what is contained in the gospel, but a subjective opening of our minds to see it. God gives the spirit of wisdom and revelation in the knowledge of him, that the eyes of our understanding being enlightened, we may know what is the hope of His calling (Eph. i. 17, 18). When the Holy Spirit thus works in us along with the gospel, we have the testimony of the Spirit in and with the word in our hearts, which gives us absolute certainty that the gospel is the word of God.

In the same way the Spirit interprets the word to us, and enables us to understand its true meaning; and this in accordance with the principles that are universally applicable in such matters. In order to understand correctly any writing, we must not only be acquainted with the language in which it is written, and the things of which it treats, but also have something in us of the spirit of the writer. Poetry, for instance, is unintelligible to those who have nothing of the poetic spirit in them, and many exquisite poems are not only unappreciated, but entirely misunderstood, by those who are destitute of imaginative feeling. So also one may read a work of philosophy, understanding the meaning of all the words and sentences, and yet have no real apprehension of the problems that are dealt with, so that the whole treatise may seem to such a one unintelligible or foolish,

In like manner the expressions of religious feelings and experiences by men like Augustine, Luther, Cromwell, or Bunyan, have often seemed insane ravings or hypocritical pretences to critics, acute enough in the judgment of worldly matters, but strangers to such deep spiritual experience. The only way in which this want of understanding can be remedied is the personal contact of soul with soul. If we not merely read or hear the words of poetry or philosophy, but have direct intercourse with a living man in whom is the poetic or philosophic spirit, we may come to have a feeling and insight into the meaning of these studies, such as we had not before ; and many can look back to a time when the understanding of poetry or of philosophy was first opened to them in some such way. Only in all such cases what is done is to awaken or call into exercise a faculty that already exists in the soul ; in the revelation of spiritual truths there is needed a power that can revive the faculty of spiritual discernment from a state in which it is practically impotent. Hence, however useful and helpful human aid may be, it must be the work of the Spirit of God to enable us really to know the things that are freely given to us by God.

This work of the Spirit is the foundation of the certainty of our faith, as resting not merely on the testimony of men but on that of God. Under His teaching we may have, not only a probable opinion, but a full assurance in regard to the things that concern our spiritual life and comfort. These are, the fact that God has spoken and does speak to us, the meaning of the message He addresses to us, and our personal interest in His promises. For none of these do we need to depend either on the authority of men, or on the inferences of reason, when we have the testimony of the Spirit of God ; though both the experience of other men, and the rational powers of our own minds, are useful as auxiliaries and confirmations of our faith.

The Holy Spirit gives us infallible assurance that God has spoken at sundry times and in divers manners by the prophets, and in the last days by His Son ; and how great a thing is it to be assured of that, so that we are not left to feel after Him in the dark by the indirect discovery of His works, but have His voice speaking personally to us! His voice indeed carries its own evidence with it; for it is worthy of Himself, divine, so that He challenges comparison with all counterfeits: "What is the chaff to the wheat? saith the LORD. Is not my word like as a fire, and like a hammer that breaketh the rock in pieces?" (Jer. xxiii. 28, 29). But unless the Spirit, through whom the word is given, open our ears to hear it, we cannot perceive this; when He does so, then we recognise the voice of God, and the saying of Jesus about Himself as the true shepherd is fulfilled, "The sheep follow him, for they know his voice, and a stranger they will not follow, for they know not the voice of strangers." The majesty, and holiness, and truthfulness, and tenderness, and grace, that shine in the word of God, the power with which it awakens the conscience and melts the heart, are demonstrations of its divine origin to those who are enabled by the Holy Spirit to perceive them; and thus by the witness of the Spirit they are assured that God does really speak to them.

But men have understood this word in so many different ways, that it seems difficult or impossible to be sure about its meaning. Hence we need a guide in the interpretation of it. Yet that is not to be sought for outside, in the teaching of the learned, or of the Church, but in the Holy Spirit enabling us to receive God's word in meekness of wisdom, and understand its plain meaning in its own light. Jesus promised that the Comforter would take of His and show it to His disciples, and the apostles pray that their converts may be enlightened by the Spirit to understand the truth. There are indeed many things in the Bible about the meaning of which competent and candid scholars doubt or differ, and probably will always do so; but these are matters of subordinate importance; and when there are differences about the main drift of its teaching, these arise from carelessness, or prejudice, or presumption: and when the Holy Spirit frees the mind from the warping influence of these, and enables us to read the word with simplicity, docility, and diligence, its meaning, as to the great essentials, is plain and certain to us.

But further, the believer receives the word of God as a personal message of God to him, and testimony of God's goodwill to him in Christ; and in this aspect of it also the Holy Spirit gives us assurance of its truth. The gospel is not indeed addressed to each individual by name, as God's words have sometimes been to the prophets; but it is addressed to men in general, and testifies to each one God's earnest desire that he should be saved from sin, and the certainty of his being saved if he will but trust in Jesus. Now if this were all, we should have a divine testimony to the general truth of the gospel, but not to our personal interest in it; that we could only learn from our own reflection or examination of ourselves. That can give us some knowledge, but it can never be absolutely certain. But along with the call of the gospel, the Holy Spirit works in our hearts, moving and enabling us to receive it in faith, and to enter into the enjoyment and appreciation of its blessings. When He thus enables us personally to return to our God, and receive His free forgiveness and reconciling love, even as the prodigal son returned to his father; when He leads us to know the peace and joy that come with such faith; when He gives us boldness to cry to God, "Our Father in heaven," can we have any doubt that God is gracious to us, and that we are reconciled to Him? Have we not a witness of this in our hearts, the witness not merely of our own consciousness or conscience, but of the Spirit of God dwelling and working in us? "The love of God is shed abroad in our hearts by the Holy Spirit which is given to us." "The Spirit itself beareth witness with our spirits that we are the children of God." "He that believeth on the Son of God hath the witness in him, . . . and the witness is this, that God gave unto us eternal life, and this life is in his Son" (Rom. v. 5, viii. 16; 1 John v. 16).

It is to be observed that this function of the Holy Spirit as our teacher and witness is not a thing distinct and apart from His general work in renewing and sanctifying our souls. He enables us to see the Scriptures to be the Word of God, to understand their true meaning, and to be assured of God's goodwill to us, and of our interest in His promises, no otherwise than by bringing our minds and hearts into sympathy and harmony with God's mind and heart as declared in His word : and that is just the work wherein our sanctification consists. To revert to the analogy before noticed, just as we come to understand and appreciate poetry or philosophy more deeply and truly, the more we grow in the poetic or philosophic spirit; so it is in proportion as we advance in Christian life in general, that we learn to perceive more easily, more correctly, and more fully, the mind of God in His word. Hence we find that enlightenment is promised in Scripture to various spiritual graces. "To him that ordereth his way aright will I show the salvation of God" (Ps. l. 23). "Unto the upright there ariseth light in the darkness" (Ps. cxii. 4). "If any man willeth to do his will, he shall know of the teaching" (John vii. 17). "Blessed are the pure in heart, for they shall see God" (Matt. v. 8). "Every one that loveth knoweth God" (1 John iv. 7). This is what secures this great truth of the testimony of the Holy Spirit from the danger of being perverted into an encouragement to fanaticism, by men mistaking the suggestions of their own fancy, or interest, or wishes, for the teaching of the Holy Spirit. If it is ever borne in mind, on the one hand that the Spirit's testimony is in and with the Word, and on the other hand that it is just a special aspect of the work of sanctification as a whole; these abuses of this doctrine may be avoided, and it may be seen to be consistent with truth and soberness, and in harmony with well-ascertained facts of our experience.

Of the way in which the Holy Spirit as a teacher is a guide to believers, in the details of practical life, and the steps they should take in various circumstances, we have a remarkable illustration in Paul's Epistles to the Corinthians, both in the advice he gives to them, and in what he says about his own plans and proceedings. They had asked his opinion on several questions of practical conduct, about marriage, about meats offered to idols, about the conduct of religious meetings, and the exercise of spiritual gifts; and he gives answers to these inquiries in successive sections of his first epistle to them. In them all he carries the question of detail in the first place up to some general principle, on which the Word of God gives a clear and authoritative decision; then he indicates how the application of this may be modified by circumstances, and how in some cases other principles come to bear upon the question, so as to define the path of duty one way or another; then he refers to various alternative suppositions, as to what might occur in actual life, and shows how the general principles of Scripture determine the right course variously in various circumstances. In each of these discussions we see lofty and comprehensive principles laid down; but then these are not left in their generality, but at the same time are so explained and applied to actual cases, that we have not mere vague commonplaces, but distinct directions capable of being applied and acted upon in practice. Now what has enabled Paul thus to combine lofty principles with precise application, is his ample acquaintance with Scripture, his clear apprehension of its real meaning, and his thorough sympathy with its spirit, and honest resolution to apply it fearlessly to varying circumstances. But these are qualities that may be possessed by ordinary Christians, without Paul's supernatural inspiration or rare intellectual gifts. If the Word of God dwell in us richly, so that we can readily perceive, when any practical question arises, what general principle Scripture has given which covers it; if we have a clear and right apprehension of the meaning of that principle, and if we are free from the tendency to apply it in a one-sided way, and are resolved honestly to decide and act upon it, then we may see how it plainly directs our path of duty: the Word of God is a lamp to our feet and a light to our path; but it is the Holy Spirit, quickening and nourishing Christian life in us, that enables us to use it as such.

Still more strikingly do we see this guidance of the Spirit in Paul's own conduct, as it comes out in these epistles. When he wrote his first epistle, he had already given up a former intention of going at once to them, from Ephesus, before the visit he had to pay to the churches in Macedonia. He made this change because he desired to make a longer stay with them (1 Cor. xvi. 5, 6); and also, as he assures them in his later letter, to spare them and give them time to reform the abuses for which he had blamed them, so that he might not have to come to them with the sorrowful duty of exercising discipline (2 Cor. i. 23–ii. 3). Thus we see how in this matter of timing his journeys he was guided by high Christian principle. The great opportunity, and at the same time the dangers of the work at Ephesus, determined him to remain there till Pentecost (1 Cor. xvi. 8, 9); but when he had left that city, his anxiety about the Corinthian Church impelled him to hurry on from Troas to Macedonia to meet Titus (2 Cor. ii. 12, 13). Here we see him led, not so much by calm consideration of duty, as by warm impulse of Christian love. Again, in the arrangements he makes about the second mission of Titus to Corinth with the delegates of the Macedonian churches, we see how Paul was guided by the high principle of providing things honourable not only in the sight of God, but also in the sight of men (2 Cor. viii. 6–21). Throughout these proceedings he was evidently guided by the general precepts of Scripture, to which he frequently refers; while we cannot but admire the clearness and practical wisdom with which he sees the application of these general precepts to the peculiar circumstances in which he was placed. We seem to see in this how he was guided by the Spirit in his Christian walk; and so, when he was accused of duplicity or indecision in his proceedings, he asserts his disinterestedness and straightforwardness, and declares that he has been enabled in this to imitate the stedfastness of Christ Himself, because God has anointed and sealed him and given the earnest of the Spirit (2 Cor. i. 19–22); while at the same time he indicates that this is not a privilege peculiar to him, but a blessing in which they and all believers may share. " He who establisheth us with you unto Christ is God."

CHAPTER IX.

THE WORK OF THE HOLY SPIRIT AS OUR HELPER IN PRAYER.

BESIDES the function of the Holy Spirit in making known to us the mind of God, there is also ascribed to Him in Scripture a special action in connection with our making known our requests to God in prayer. We have the promise of the spirit of grace and of supplications (Zech. xii. 10); the Spirit is said to help our infirmities in the exercise of prayer, and to make intercession for us (Rom. viii. 26, 27); the Spirit is said to cry in our hearts, Abba, Father (Gal. iv. 6); and we are exhorted to pray in the Holy Spirit (Jude 20).

In the first of these passages there is no reason to believe that the prophet had the idea of a personal divine agent; it is rather a disposition or tendency in the human soul that is suggested by his words. But it is a disposition of a truly religious and devotional nature, including love or kindness in the heart, and the outcome of that in humble petitions for pardon and blessing; and this frame of mind is promised to be given by God, and to be such as to lead to a thorough conversion of the people from ungodliness and idolatry. Even here therefore we can hardly fail to see, that true prayer is represented as a special result of that renewing work of God in the souls of men, which we learn in the New Testament to ascribe especially to the Holy Spirit. In so far as he implants and nourishes in us the new life of faith, repentance, and love, the Spirit of God stimulates and helps the exercise of prayer; for that is, as it were, the breath of the new life, the natural and spontaneous action of it. Like every exercise of spiritual life, prayer presupposes the existence of that life itself, and it will be energetic and abundant in proportion as the life is healthful and strong. So, as that life both in its beginning and in its continuance and growth, depends on the power of the Holy Spirit, the habit and activity of prayer may be traced to His agency. "Quicken us, and we will call upon thy name," must ever be the language of God's people.

But the New Testament seems to point to a more special connection of the Holy Spirit with the prayers of believers in Jesus. In the same chapter in which he speaks of the Spirit bearing witness with our spirits that we are children of God, Paul says that the Spirit also helps our infirmities in the way of prayer. The infirmity here specially in the apostle's view is our ignorance, not our disinclination to come to God in prayer: the remedy for that he had spoken of before, when he said that we "have received the Spirit of adoption, whereby we cry, Abba, Father" (Rom. viii. 15). But even when we are enabled thus to address God as our Father, we may be at a loss in prayer, from want of knowing what we should pray for as we ought. We know that we need much for our complete salvation; we have been saved in hope, but not yet in full fruition; we feel the evils that beset and surround us; and we are assured by our faith in Christ that these shall yet be entirely removed; but what really are the roots of these evils, or in what way we are to look and labour for their removal, we do not distinctly know. In our ignorance and confusion, we may often be apt to pray for the removal of what is really for our good, or for the bestowal of things that would be pernicious. Hence we need the aid of the Holy Spirit. But He helps us, not by revealing to us precisely what we should ask for in each particular emergency, but by securing that our groanings, even though they cannot be articulately expressed, shall serve the purpose of prayer. The Spirit makes intercession for us with these very groanings that cannot be uttered; that is, He not only prompts them, but presents them to God in such a way that they are heard and answered. He who is the hearer of prayer searches the hearts, and does not need that their desires should be expressed in words, in order that He may know what they are; and when they are wrought by His own Spirit in the hearts of those who are His own people, His holy ones, He knows that they are according to His will. Thus, since the Holy Spirit, dwelling in us and moving us to prayer, is ever in fellowship and union with the Father and the Son; our desires, however confused and inarticulate they may be in our consciousness, are yet the expression of the mind of the Spirit, and so are acceptable and prevailing prayers. To offer up our desires to God, under the influence of the Spirit, and trusting to His intercession, seems to be what is meant by praying in the Holy Spirit (Jude, 20), crying by, or in, the Spirit, Abba, Father (Rom. viii. 15), having access through Christ by, or in, one Spirit unto the Father (Eph. ii. 18). Again, as the mystical connection of the believer with the Spirit is variously expressed, now by saying that he is in the Spirit, and again that the Spirit is in him; so this agency of the Holy Spirit is also described as His crying in us, "Abba, Father" (Gal. iv. 6). The prayers of the children of God, and even their inarticulate longings after the full accomplishment of salvation, are utterances of the will of the Spirit of God, who is one with the Father and the Son in the wonderful purpose of love from which salvation springs.

In this function of the Holy Spirit, as making intercession for us, we may see, more distinctly than in any other of His works, the meaning and importance of the scriptural statements about the Spirit not merely working, but dwelling in believers. As before observed, these statements cannot refer to the essential presence of the Spirit of God, for being divine, that is everywhere; but they denote that the Holy Spirit works in the souls of Christians in a way that He does not work in those of others. Yet it is not merely the works of the Spirit, or the gracious feelings and inclinations wrought by Him, that we mean, when we speak of, or pray for, the indwelling of the Spirit. Were this all that is promised and granted to us, it might indeed, for ought we know, be sufficient for our faith and holiness; but on that supposition it could not be said in any natural sense, that the Holy Spirit made intercession for us. That action implies personality and personal agency; and so we must conclude that not merely the gifts or operations of the Spirit, but the Spirit Himself is given and sent into our hearts. Whatever difficulty there may be in forming a conception of how this is so, this is the meaning obviously suggested by our Lord's promises in the farewell discourses recorded by John; and although He does not there speak of the Spirit making intercession for them, He gives that view of the Spirit as a person, which makes His intercession intelligible; and when He calls Him another Comforter or Advocate, who is to supply His place, and remain with His disciples always, He at least suggests this as one of His functions.

The evidence to individual Christians of the Spirit's help and intercession in their prayers is not always their freedom and fluency of expression, or their comfort and delight in the exercise, or their fervour and rapture of devotion. All these may sometimes be due to natural causes, or to baseless imagination; and they may sometimes be absent when there is really prayer in the Holy Spirit. The only true and unfailing test of His assistance is the accordance of the prayer with the mind of God. That includes two things: for as prayer is essentially the offering up of our desires to God, it is needful that the desires themselves be right, and that they be offered up aright. By renewing and sanctifying our affections, the Holy Spirit secures that our desires are for things agreeable to God's will, moving us to seek His face and favour as our chief good, and raising us above mere selfish and worldly inclinations. When we are desiring holiness, and hating sin, longing for the glory of God and the truest good of our fellowmen, and wishing temporal comforts and happiness only in subordination to these ends, and as far as they conduce to them, then our desires are in harmony with God's will, and as such desires are not natural or spontaneous in the heart of any unrenewed man, and even in the heart of the renewed have to contend with many opposing tendencies, we may be sure that where they really exist, in however small a degree, the Holy Spirit has been their author, and so is helping to pray.

But it is as necessary for acceptable prayer, that the desires be offered to God aright, as that they be right in themselves. They are to be offered in the name of Christ, with confession of our sins, and thankful acknowledgment of God's mercies. Now, these things are all involved in Christian faith, and are secured if we have faith in Christ as He is offered to us in the gospel. For that implies, that we feel and acknowledge that we are sinners, guilty and inexcusable, and that any good that we enjoy is altogether undeserved and of God's free mercy; that we have and express humble thankfulness to Him for all the benefits He bestows; and that we trust in Christ for forgiveness, and all blessings that we need and ask in prayer. Such sentiments and convictions as these are the work of the Holy Spirit moving and enabling us to repentance and faith; and to pray under the influence and impression of them is to pray in the Holy Spirit. But as these convictions are in their nature of a humbling and self-abasing tendency, the aid of the Holy Spirit in prayer may oftentimes appear in the intense grief, self-loathing, and self-distrust with which our petitions are offered. Thus Zechariah describes the pouring out of the spirit of grace and of supplications as leading to the bitterest mourning; and Paul speaks of the Spirit making intercession for us with unutterable groanings. The Spirit indeed always prompts the childlike cry, "Abba, Father;" and thus gives confidence, even when we are most cast down; often too His help in devotion may be seen in the freedom, and delight, and hopefulness with which we are enabled to make known our requests to God; but we are not to suppose that when these joyful feelings are absent, we are without His assistance. The true test is the holiness and the faith with which we pray.

CHAPTER X.

THE COMFORTING WORK OF THE HOLY SPIRIT.

ALTHOUGH the name Comforter, by which we render the title Paraclete or Advocate, given to the Spirit by Jesus, must be understood to include many more functions besides what we generally mean by comfort; yet there can be no doubt that it does comprehend the narrower use of the word, in the sense of giving consolation in trouble or sorrow; and there are other passages of Scripture that describe the agency of the Holy Spirit in this special way. We must not indeed separate this part of His work from the others; for indeed one great lesson that we should learn from all our consideration of the work of the Holy Spirit is, that no part of it can be isolated from the others, and that the various functions that we ascribe to Him, of convincing, converting, sanctifying, witnessing, interceding, and comforting are rather different aspects of one and the same great work. We cannot study deeply any one of the special works of the Spirit, without finding that it rests upon His agency in creating and fostering spiritual life in the soul, and is but a special form or application of that work. Yet we do well to consider distinctly these several aspects of the Spirit's work in us; for not only are they all suited to our several wants, but each reveals a special aspect of the Holy Spirit Himself. Thus His converting and sanctifying work especially illustrates His power and His holiness; His function as a witness shows His truth and faithfulness;

and above all His agency as the Comforter reveals His love. For this work has to do with men considered as liable to dejection, trouble, and sorrow ; and has for its object to relieve these painful affections, and to fill our souls with joy. Now this can proceed from nothing but love, desiring and delighting in the happiness of the loved ones. The deliverance of men from actual danger of perishing may be due simply to pity or compassion ; their sanctification may be due to a love of holiness; but to seek their comfort is sure evidence of love. Out of mere pity one might procure the release of a criminal from prison; out of zeal for virtue one might labour to reform him ; but both these ends might be secured though nothing were done to relieve him from sad feelings of gloom and self-reproach, and to make his life positively happy ; and if one were found caring for this too, and taking pains to comfort and cheer him, this would show, that such a benefactor was moved, not merely by general philanthropy, but by personal affection. So, when the Holy Spirit is revealed in Scripture as not only saving and sanctifying us, but undertaking the office of a Comforter, to fill us with joy and peace, we see in this a most wonderful evidence of His love.

This office the Holy Spirit performs partly by presenting to our minds the objects best fitted to give encouragement and comfort, especially the person and work of Christ, and the grace and faithfulness of God therein revealed. This is what Jesus speaks of the Spirit as doing, when He promised Him as a Comforter to supply His place. "He shall teach you all things, and bring to your remembrance all that I said unto you ;" "He shall bear witness of me ;" "He shall glorify me, for He shall take of mine and declare it unto you" (John xiv. 26, xv. 26, xvi. 14). This is a particular aspect of His work as a witness, of which Jesus speaks more generally. His testimony to the ungodly and unbelieving world is also of Christ, but is such as to produce conviction of sin, and so awaken feelings of distress, anxiety, and alarm. But the person and work of Christ are the only things that can give real comfort to the soul in a religious point of view, and hence to those who look to Christ in faith, this work of the Holy Spirit is truly one of consolation. In giving us ever clearer views and more certain convictions of what Jesus is and has done as our Saviour, the Spirit acts as our Comforter.

But He also performs this work inwardly, inasmuch as peace, and joy, and hope, which form the elements of comfort, are the effects of His presence and work in the soul. We read of the disciples who heard in faith the tidings of the grace of God being filled with joy and the Holy Spirit (Acts xiii. 52); and of the Thessalonians, to whom the gospel came in power, and in the Holy Spirit, and in much assurance, receiving it with joy of the Holy Spirit (1 Thess. i. 5, 6). Paul includes in the fruit of the Spirit joy and peace (Gal. v. 22), and declares the kingdom of God to be righteousness, and peace, and joy in the Holy Spirit (Rom. xiv. 17), and prays that God would fill his readers with all joy and peace in believing, that they may abound in hope by the power of the Holy Spirit (Rom. xv. 13). These passages show that joy is not merely the effect of the truths of the gospel, of which the Holy Spirit gives us evidence, but a direct exercise of that new life in the soul, of which the Holy Spirit is the author. Nor is this a thing hard to explain. Joy is an element of healthy religious life, without which it would be defective. It is right and proper for one who is a child, under the care of an all-wise and loving God, not only to adore and love and trust his Father in heaven, but also to rejoice in thinking of His greatness, His goodness, His love. Indeed, there cannot be genuine religious feeling without some measure of that delight in God that is so often expressed in the devotional utterances of Scripture. If then the Spirit of God produces in us that life of devotion, there cannot but be awakened, as a part of it, holy and religious joy. Thus the Holy Spirit is our Comforter, not only by presenting to us those objects that are fitted to dispel grief and fear, and cause joy and hope, but also by inwardly moving us to cherish and exercise holy joy. The former function is connected with His work as a Teacher and Witness, the latter with His work as the Author and

Nourisher of spiritual life. This twofold function may also explain the striking language of Scripture about the sealing and the earnest of the Spirit.

When the figure of sealing is used in this connection, it is God who is said to have sealed believers in Christ with the Holy Spirit (2 Cor. i. 22; Eph. i. 13, iv. 30). In the first of these passages, a parallel is drawn between Christ and His followers primarily in regard to stability or constancy of purpose, and then also in regard to those spiritual endowments that produce that constancy. Paul s defending himself against the charge of duplicity or fickleness, of wavering in promise or purpose from yea to nay. He affirms that he had not done so, because Christ, whom he proclaimed as the Son of God, had not done so; and God had made him, and his readers too, stedfast, had established them unto Christ. In allusion to the meaning of that title, he adds, that God had anointed them also, and sealed them. This reminds us of Jesus saying of Himself, "Him the Father, even God, hath sealed" (John vi. 27). That was the assurance He gave to the people that they might safely trust Him for the food which abideth unto eternal life. Now as the Holy Spirit is elsewhere compared by Jesus to food (Luke xi. 11–13), and as we are taught that Jesus was able to baptize with the Holy Spirit, because the Spirit descended and abode on Him; we are led to regard the sealing He speaks of having received as referring to the gift and manifestation of the Holy Spirit on Him. The sealing in His case was chiefly a testimony to others, though doubtless also to His own human soul; in the case of believers it is mainly for their own encouragement that the seal of the Spirit is referred to.

The special use of sealing, to which allusion is made in these applications of the idea, both to Christ and to Christians, seems to be that of marking property to which the owner attaches value, but which may be in danger of being neglected or lost. When God sent His Son into the world, the world knew Him not, and sought for a sign that they might believe. Jesus said, that the Father had borne witness to Him, and sealed Him, and so marked Him out as His own, doing the works of God in the power of His Spirit. So too God takes those who believe in Christ to be His special possession, which He has purchased or obtained for Himself.[1] But they are not at once taken out of the world, but left in it, often unknown and unesteemed by men. Meanwhile God has marked them for His own, as men mark valued property, with the seal of His Spirit until the time when He shall openly take them to Himself in full possession. This idea is also implied in the use made of the figure of sealing the servants of God in the Apocalyptic vision (Rev. vii. 1-8, ix. 4), that they may be marked as those who are to be spared in impending judgments (compare also Ezek. ix. 4-6); but there is no indication to connect that sealing especially with the work of the Spirit. The Pauline idea of the sealing of believers by the Spirit may possibly bear an allusion to the restoration of the image of God through Christ, who is said in Heb. i. 3 to be the very image of His substance (lit. impress or stamp, as on a seal); but it is not to be identified with the progressive work of moral renewal; for it is always described as done at once, and when we believe. It is therefore rather that spiritual or religious likeness and affinity to Christ, that is a token of real union to Him, even where there is much imperfection of moral character; that trustful love and loyalty that shows a heart right with God amid much that is sinful in conduct. Such was the love of the sinful woman who washed Jesus' feet with her tears (Luke vii. 36-50); such that of Simon Peter even after he had denied his Master in the hour of temptation (John xxi. 15-17). So also Paul speaks of bearing branded on his body the marks of Jesus (Gal. vi. 17), in the scars of his stripes and wounds for Jesus' sake, which gave evidence, not of his moral perfection, but of his loyalty and love to his Lord. This unmistakable seal of

---

[1] The word "purchased" is used in the Authorized Version of the Bible in its old sense, from the French *pourchasser*, to chase after, to obtain for oneself, without necessarily implying the payment of a price. So Shakspeare uses it: "I sent thee forth to purchase honour" (*Rich. II.*, Act I. Sc. 3).

true godliness is what distinguishes such a man as David, with strong unruly passions, that often hurried him into great crimes of sensuality and cruelty, but with as passionate a devotion to God, repentance for sin, and longing for purity as well as pardon, from one like Saul less outwardly guilty, but cold, timid, and worldly. "The Lord hath set apart him that is godly for himself," one whom He favoureth, and who responds to that favour in the prayer of childlike trust (Ps. iv. 3). While many who profess and seem to be godly give way before error and temptation, the firm foundation of God abides, the people whom He has built on Christ the foundation-stone, having the twofold seal: "The Lord knoweth them that are his," and, "Let every one that nameth the name of the Lord depart from unrighteousness" (2 Tim. ii. 19). In writing thus, Paul had probably in his mind the narrative of the rebellion of Korah (Num. xvi.), where it is said on the one hand (v. 5), "In the morning the Lord will show who are his, and who is holy, and will cause him to come near unto him;" and on the other hand (v. 26), "Depart, I pray you, from the tents of these wicked men, and touch nothing of theirs, lest ye be consumed in all their sins." They who act in the spirit of these two sayings, have the seal of God marking them as the people whom He has made His own, and will finally deliver from all evil; and the Holy Spirit enabling them so to do, seals them unto the day of redemption.

The Spirit whereby they are thus sealed is also the earnest of the inheritance destined for them (2 Cor. i. 22, v. 5; Eph. i. 14[1]). An earnest is not only a pledge but a foretaste or anticipation of the benefit secured by the pledge; and when this name is given

---

[1] The word translated "earnest" in these places is the same that is rendered "pledge" in Gen. xxxviii. 17-20; indeed the Hebrew word has simply passed into the Greek and Latin languages, probably through commercial dealings with the Phœnicians, the great trading people of ancient days. Originally it meant no more than a pledge; but in usage it came to denote that particular kind of pledge which is a part of the full price of an article paid in advance; and as it is joined with the figure of a seal when applied to the Spirit, it seems to be used by Paul in this specific sense.

to the Holy Spirit, we are taught that His gracious presence and working in us constitute a foretaste of the blessedness of heaven. The same thing seems to be indicated when Paul speaks of the first-fruits of the Spirit (Rom. viii. 23), which is most naturally interpreted as meaning the Spirit as the first-fruits of glory. These representations refer to the Holy Spirit as the source of joy and peace. The sealing of the Spirit may often be not joyous, but painful; it may imply a self-denying departing from iniquity, or an endurance of suffering for Christ's sake; the chastisements of our heavenly Father are pledges of the blessing He has in store for His children, though in themselves they are of an opposite nature. But He who knows our frame, and remembers that we are dust, is graciously pleased to give us, not only pledges of future blessedness, but foretastes of it also. The former appeal to our faith, and may be even painful to our sensibilities: the atter are necessarily joyful, and are meant for our comfort.

This truth, that the joy of the Holy Spirit is a beginning of the blessedness of heaven, is of great practical use, as a safeguard against dreamy and fanciful ideas, that may even degenerate into earthly and sensual expectations of future bliss. There is ever a danger of this when we regard the joy that is set before us as something of which we have no experience here. It will in that case be either entirely vague and indistinct, or we shall introduce into our thoughts of it those enjoyments of this world that we have to deny to ourselves for the sake of Christ, and we shall simply hope to be recompensed in a future life for the sacrifices made in this. If however we have any experience of a holy joy, even amid the sins and sorrows of this world; if we know in any measure what Peter meant when he said, that believing in Christ we rejoice with joy unspeakable and full of glory, and what Paul meant when he spoke of rejoicing in tribulations, and rejoicing in God through Jesus Christ our Lord; then we can form a conception of one element at least in the future blessedness that is not in the least degree earthly or sensuous. We have also a strong assurance of the truth and certainty of our hope. It promises us nothing different in kind from what we already enjoy imperfectly, though in degree something inconceivably more pure and perfect. Here it may only be fitfully and in snatches that we have, or believe that we have, something of the joy of the Holy Spirit: we hardly dare trust ourselves to enjoy it; and we are encompassed and interrupted with much that humiliates, pains, tempts, and wearies us. We just know enough of this holy joy to make us feel how real it is, and to give us a faint idea how great must be the blessedness when it is perfect, unalloyed, and unbroken. The Spirit that makes Christians happy in the midst of shame and suffering is called the Spirit of glory and of God (1 Pet. iv. 14), as the Spirit who possesses the glory of God, who glorifies Christ, and will glorify all who are Christ's. This title is an appropriate sequel to that of the spirit of grace, for glory is but grace perfected, as grace is glory begun. He is the Spirit of grace, as beginning the new life in the sorrows of self-accusing repentance; and the Spirit of glory as completing it, in the joy of the open manifestation and glorious liberty of the sons of God.

'A most useful series of Handbooks. With such helps as these, to be an inefficient teacher is to be blameworthy.'—Rev. C. H. SPURGEON.

BIBLE CLASS PRIMERS.

Edited by Rev. Professor SALMOND, D.D.

In paper covers, 6d. each; free by post, 7d. In cloth, 8d. each; free by post, 9d.

Outlines of Protestant Missions.
By JOHN ROBSON, D.D.

Life of the Apostle Peter.
By Rev. Professor SALMOND, D.D.
'A work which only an accomplished scholar could have produced.'—*Christian Leader*.

Outlines of Early Church History.
By Rev. HENRY WALLIS SMITH, D.D.
'An admirable sketch of early Church history.'—*Baptist*.

Life of David.   12th Thousand.
By the late Rev. PETER THOMSON, M.A.
'I think it is excellent indeed, and have seen nothing of the kind so good.'—Rev. STANLEY LEATHES, D.D.

Life of Moses.   20th Thousand.
By Rev. JAMES IVERACH, M.A.
'Accurately done, clear, mature, and scholarly.'—*Christian*.

Life of Paul.   10th Thousand.
By PATON J. GLOAG, D.D.
'This little book could not well be surpassed.'—*Daily Review*.

Life and Reign of Solomon.   10th Thousand.
By Rev. RAYNER WINTERBOTHAM, M.A., LL.B.
'Every teacher should have it.'—Rev. C. H. SPURGEON.

The History of the Reformation.   6th Thousand.
By Rev. Professor WITHEROW.
'A vast amount of information set forth in a clear and concise manner.'—*United Presbyterian Magazine*.

The Kings of Israel.   5th Thousand.
By Rev. W. WALKER, M.A.
'A masterpiece of lucid condensation.'—*Christian Leader*.

The Kings of Judah.   5th Thousand.
By Rev. Professor GIVEN, Ph.D.
'Admirably arranged; the style is sufficiently simple and clear to be quite within the compass of young people.'—*British Messenger*.

Joshua and the Conquest.   5th Thousand.
By Rev. Professor CROSKERY.
'This carefully written manual will be much appreciated.'—*Daily Review*.

Bible Words and Phrases, Explained and Illustrated.
By Rev. CHARLES MICHIE, M.A.   18mo, cloth, 1s.
'Will be found interesting and instructive, and of the greatest value to young students and teachers.'—*Athenæum*.

T. and T. Clark's Publications.

Just published, in crown 8vo, price 6s.,

OLD AND NEW THEOLOGY:
A CONSTRUCTIVE CRITIQUE.

BY REV. J. B. HEARD, M.A.

'We can promise all real students of Holy Scripture who have found their way out of some of the worst of the scholastic byelanes and ruts, and are striving to reach the broad and firm high road that leads to the Eternal City, a real treat from the perusal of these pages. Progressive theologians, who desire to find "the old in the new, and the new in the old," will be deeply grateful to Mr. Heard for this courageous and able work.'—*Christian World.*

'Among the many excellent theological works, whether English or German, published by Messrs. Clark, there are few that deserve more careful study than this book. . . . It cannot fail to charm by its grace of style, and to supply food for solid thought.'—*Dublin Express.*

BY THE SAME AUTHOR.

Fifth Edition, in crown 8vo, price 6s.,

THE TRIPARTITE NATURE OF MAN:
SPIRIT, SOUL, AND BODY.

Applied to Illustrate and Explain the Doctrines of Original Sin, the New Birth, the Disembodied State, and the Spiritual Body.

'The author has got a striking and consistent theory. Whether agreeing or disagreeing with that theory, it is a book which any student of the Bible may read with pleasure.'—*Guardian.*

'An elaborate, ingenious, and very able book.'—*London Quarterly Review.*

Just published, in demy 8vo, price 9s.,

THE DOCTRINE OF THE HOLY SPIRIT.
(The Ninth Series of the Cunningham Lectures.)

BY GEORGE SMEATON, D.D.,

Professor of Exegetical Theology, New College, Edinburgh.

'The theological student will be benefited by a careful perusal of this survey, and that not for the moment, but through all his future life.'—*Watchman.*

'Very cordially do we commend these able and timely lectures to the notice of our readers. Every theological student should master them.'—*Baptist Magazine.*

'It is a pleasure to meet with a work like this. . . . Our brief account, we trust, will induce the desire to study this work.'—*Dickinson's Theological Quarterly.*

T. and T. Clark's Publications.

In crown 8vo, price 6s.,

CHRISTIAN CHARITY IN THE ANCIENT CHURCH.

By G. UHLHORN, D.D.

Translated with the Author's sanction.

'A very excellent translation of a very valuable book.'—*Guardian.*'

'This book is a careful and learned monograph on a subject which is always interesting.'—*Academy.*

'It is without hesitation that we recommend this admirable treatise, which will amply repay perusal. Its intention is excellent, its subject momentous, its arguments are solid, its style winning, and its learning beyond dispute.'—*Tablet.*

In demy 8vo, price 9s.,

LECTURES,

CHIEFLY EXPOSITORY,
ON
ST. PAUL'S EPISTLES TO THE THESSALONIANS.

With Notes and Illustrations.

By JOHN HUTCHISON, D.D.

'We have read this book with real interest, and we are sure that it will furnish much help to clergymen who may undertake the work of expository preaching, and that both clergymen and laymen will find it helpful and edifying.'—*Church Bells.*

'Models of pulpit exposition. . . . Would that we had many expositions as thoughtful and scholarly as Dr. Hutchison's.'—*Methodist Recorder.*

'To the working minister this work supplies an admirable model, and to the unprofessional reader it will be pleasant and profitable for instruction.'—*Outlook.*

In ex. demy vo, price 12s.,

THE PHILOSOPHICAL BASIS OF THEISM:

AN EXAMINATION OF THE PERSONALITY OF MAN TO ASCERTAIN HIS CAPACITY TO KNOW AND SERVE GOD, AND THE VALIDITY OF THE PRINCIPLES UNDERLYING THE DEFENCE OF THEISM.

By SAMUEL HARRIS, D.D., LL.D.

'The whole volume will be found, by all who are interested in its subject, full of suggestive thought, and of real assistance in unfolding to the mind the true account and justification of its religious knowledge.'—*Spectator.*

'The course pursued by the author of this book is a very exhaustive and satisfactory one. . . . His book is a singularly able treatise on the subject, and a kind of cyclopædia of reference to its literature.'—*Courant.*

T. and T. Clark's Publications.

Just published, in crown 8vo, price 3s. 6d.,

THE RELIGIOUS HISTORY OF ISRAEL.

A DISCUSSION OF THE CHIEF PROBLEMS IN OLD TESTAMENT HISTORY, AS OPPOSED TO THE DEVELOPMENT THEORISTS.

By Dr. FRIEDRICH EDUARD KÖNIG.

TRANSLATED BY REV. ALEXANDER J. CAMPBELL, M.A.

'An admirable little volume. . . . By sincere and earnest-minded students it will be cordially welcomed.'—*Freeman.*

'Every page of the book deserves study.'—*Church Bells.*

Just published, in crown 8vo, price 6s.,

PASTORAL THEOLOGY IN THE NEW TESTAMENT.

By J. T. BECK, D.D.

EDITED BY PROFESSOR RIGGENBACH.

TRANSLATED BY REV. JAMES M'CLYMONT, B.D., AND REV. THOMAS NICOL, B.D.

'A most valuable study for students and young ministers.'—*Nonconformist.*

'An interesting exposition of the teaching of Scripture on the subject of the Pastoral Office.'—*Spectator.*

'The volume contains much which any thoughtful and earnest Christian minister will find helpful and suggestive to him for the wise and efficient discharge of his sacred functions.'—*Literary World.*

NEW EXPOSITORY MAGAZINE.

One Shilling Monthly. Annual Subscription (free by post), 12s., if prepaid.

Now ready, price 7s. 6d. each,

VOLUMES I., II.,

THE MONTHLY INTERPRETER.

EDITED BY REV. JOS. S. EXELL, M.A.,

Vicar of Dartmouth; Joint-Editor, 'Pulpit Commentary.'

PAPERS by the following Eminent Writers appear in these Volumes:—

Rev. Canon RAWLINSON, Rev. Prebendary HUXTABLE, Rev. Prebendary GIBSON, Rev. WILLIAM J. DEANE, M.A., Professor BRUCE, D.D., T. K. CHEYNE, D.D., THOMAS WHITELAW, D.D., GEORGE MATHESON, D.D., Rev. Professor SAYCE, Rev. Professor JOHNSON, M.A., Rev. D. M. ROSS, M.A., Rev. Principal DOUGLAS, D.D., JAMES MORISON, D.D., JOHN HUTCHISON, D.D., JOSEPH JOHN MURPHY, Professor MILLIGAN, D.D., Rev. Professor REDFORD, etc.

'Mr. Exell is to be congratulated on the appearance of this the first volume of a new periodical of Scripture exegesis. He has gathered around him an excellent company of assistants and contributors, and there is every promise of the "Monthly Interpreter" being a valuable addition to Biblical literature.'—*Spectator.*

T. and T. Clark's Publications.

In Two Volumes, ex. 8vo, price 21s.,

THE DOCTRINE OF SACRED SCRIPTURE:

A CRITICAL, HISTORICAL, AND DOGMATIC INQUIRY INTO THE ORIGIN AND NATURE OF THE OLD AND NEW TESTAMENTS.

By GEORGE T. LADD, D.D.

' This work is one which will certainly be studied by all scientific theologians, and the general reader will probably find here a better summary of the whole subject than in any other work or series of works.'—*Church Bells.*

' This important work is pre-eminently adapted for students, and treats in an exhaustive manner nearly every important subject of Biblical criticism which is agitating the religious mind at the present day.'—*Contemporary Review.*

' These massive volumes give us the most extensive, elaborate, and thoroughgoing work upon this doctrine which has ever been produced. . . . The author had made years of preparation for his work. He was determined to accomplish it thoroughly. He has endeavoured to be exhaustive, and as complete as human work can be.'—*Presbyterian Review.*

In ex. crown 8vo, price 7s. 6d.,

BIBLICAL STUDY;

ITS PRINCIPLES, METHODS, AND HISTORY.

Together with a Catalogue of Books of Reference.

By C. A. BRIGGS, D.D.

With Introduction by A. B. BRUCE, D.D.

' The style glows with a fervour and eloquence which reminds us of the earlier Reformers. One's feelings are not ruffled by any traces of pedantry, and one rises from the book with the feeling that we have been dealing with a writer of the most transparent honesty, and whose free excursions are perhaps all the bolder because he refuses to break with the historic symbols, upon the broad interpretation of which he feels himself strong, against both the dogmatism of the schools and the narrow interpretations of popular theology.'—*British Quarterly Review.*

' Dr. Briggs is one of the ablest, most learned, and in the best sense most progressive of the younger Biblical scholars of America. . . . In an eminent degree he combines the historical spirit with its reverence and learning, and the scientific spirit with its freedom and candour. . . . We have great pleasure in recommending his work to the notice of all Biblical students.'—*Nonconformist.*

' Written by one who has made himself a master of the subject, and who is able to write upon it both with the learning of the scholar and the earnestness of sincere conviction. . . . Is deserving of a cordial reception from Biblical students in this country.'—*Scotsman.*

HISTORY OF THE CHRISTIAN CHURCH.
By PHILIP SCHAFF, D.D., LL.D.

A New Edition thoroughly Revised and Enlarged.

Now Ready,

APOSTOLIC CHRISTIANITY, A.D. 1–100. In Two Vols. ex. demy 8vo, price 21s.

ANTE-NICENE CHRISTIANITY, A.D. 100–311. In Two Vols. ex. demy 8vo, price 21s.

NICENE AND POST-NICENE CHRISTIANITY, A.D. 311–600. In Two Vols. ex. demy 8vo, price 21s.

MEDIÆVAL CHRISTIANITY, A.D. 590–1073. In Two Vols. ex. 8vo, price 21s.

'For a genuine healthy Christian criticism, which boldly faces difficulties, and examines them with equal candour and learning, we commend this work to all who are interested in investigating the early growth of the Christian Church.'—*Church Quarterly Review.*

'These volumes cannot fail to prove welcome to all students.'—*Freeman.*

'No student, and indeed no critic, can with fairness overlook a work like the present, written with such evident candour, and, at the same time, with so thorough a knowledge of the sources of early Christian history.'—*Scotsman.*

In Three Volumes, demy 8vo, price 12s. each,

A HISTORY OF THE COUNCILS OF THE CHURCH.
FROM THE ORIGINAL DOCUMENTS.

TRANSLATED FROM THE GERMAN OF

C. J. HEFELE, D.D., BISHOP OF ROTTENBURG.

VOL. I. (*Second Edition*) TO A.D. 325.
By REV. PREBENDARY CLARK.

VOL. II. A.D. 326 TO 429.
By H. N. OXENHAM, M.A.

VOL. III. A.D. 429 TO THE CLOSE OF THE COUNCIL OF CHALCEDON.

'This careful translation of Hefele's Councils.'—Dr. PUSEY.

'A thorough and fair compendium, put in a most accessible and intelligent form.'—*Guardian.*

'A work of profound erudition, and written in a most candid spirit. The book will be a standard work on the subject.'—*Spectator.*

'The most learned historian of the Councils.'—*Père Gratry.*

'We cordially commend Hefele's Councils to the English student.'—*John Bull.*

T. and T. Clark's Publications.

In Twenty-four handsome 8vo Volumes, Subscription price £6, 6s.,

ANTE-NICENE CHRISTIAN LIBRARY.

A COLLECTION OF ALL THE WORKS OF THE FATHERS OF THE CHRISTIAN CHURCH PRIOR TO THE COUNCIL OF NICÆA.

EDITED BY THE

Rev. ALEXANDER ROBERTS, D.D., and JAMES DONALDSON, LL.D.

CONTENTS:—Apostolic Fathers, one vol.; Justin Martyr, Athenagoras, one vol.; Tatian, Theophilus, The Clementine Recognitions, one vol.; Clement of Alexandria, two vols.; Irenæus and Hippolytus, three vols.; Tertullian against Marcion; Cyprian, two vols.; Origen, two vols.; Tertullian, three vols.; Methodius, etc., one vol.; Apocryphal Gospels, Acts, and Revelations, one vol.; Clementine Homilies, Apostolical Constitutions, one vol.; Arnobius, one vol.; Dionysius, Gregory Thaumaturgus, Syrian Fragments, one vol.; Lactantius, two vols.; Early Liturgies and Remaining Fragments, one vol.

Any Volume may be had separately, price 10s. 6d.,—with the exception of ORIGEN. Vol. II., 12s.; *and the* EARLY LITURGIES, 9s.

In Fifteen Volumes, demy 8vo, Subscription price £3, 19s.,

THE WORKS OF ST. AUGUSTINE.

EDITED BY MARCUS DODS, D.D.

CONTENTS:—The 'City of God,' two vols.; Writings in connection with the Donatist Controversy, one vol.; The Anti-Pelagian Writings, three vols.; 'Letters,' two vols.; Treatises against Faustus the Manichæan, one vol.; The Harmony of the Evangelists, and the Sermon on the Mount, one vol.; On the Trinity, one vol.; Commentary on John, two vols.; On Christian Doctrine, Enchiridion, On Catechizing, and On Faith and the Creed, one vol.; 'Confessions,' with Copious Notes by Rev. J. G. PILKINGTON.

Any Work may be had separately, price 10s. 6d. per Volume.

SELECTION FROM ANTE-NICENE LIBRARY AND ST. AUGUSTINE'S WORKS.

THE Ante-Nicene Library being now completed in 24 Volumes, and the St. Augustine Series being also complete (*with the exception of the* 'LIFE') in 15 Volumes, Messrs. CLARK will, as in the case of the Foreign Theological Library, give a Selection of 20 Volumes from both of those series at the *Subscription price* of FIVE GUINEAS (or a larger number at same proportion).

LANGE'S COMMENTARIES.

(Subscription price, nett) 15s. each.

THEOLOGICAL AND HOMILETICAL COMMENTARY ON THE OLD AND NEW TESTAMENTS. Specially designed and adapted for the use of Ministers and Students. By Prof. JOHN PETER LANGE, D.D., in connection with a number of eminent European Divines. Translated, enlarged, and revised under the general editorship of Rev. Dr. PHILIP SCHAFF, assisted by leading Divines of the various Evangelical Denominations.

OLD TESTAMENT—14 VOLUMES.

1. **Genesis.** With a General Introduction to the Old Testament. By Prof. J. P. LANGE, D.D. Translated from the German, with Additions, by Prof TAYLER LEWIS, LL.D., and A. GOSMAN, D.D.
2. **Exodus.** By J. P. LANGE, D.D. **Leviticus.** By J. P. LANGE, D.D. With GENERAL INTRODUCTION by Rev. Dr. OSGOOD.
3. **Numbers and Deuteronomy.**—Numbers. By Prof. J. P. LANGE, D.D Deuteronomy. By W. J. SCHROEDER.
4. **Joshua.** By Rev. F. R. FAY. **Judges and Ruth.** By Prof. PAULUS CASSELL, D.D.
5. **Samuel, I. and II.** By Professor ERDMANN, D.D.
6. **Kings.** By KARL CHR. W. F. BAHR, D.D.
7. **Chronicles, I. and II.** By OTTO ZÖCKLER. **Ezra.** By FR. W. SCHULTZ. **Nehemiah** By Rev. HOWARD CROSBY, D.D., LL.D. **Esther.** By FR. W. SCHULTZ.
8. **Job.** With an Introduction and Annotations by Prof. TAYLER LEWIS, LL.D. A Commentary by Dr. OTTO ZOCKLER, together with an Introductory Essay on Hebrew Poetry by Prof. PHILIP SCHAFF, D.D.
9. **The Psalms.** By CARL BERNHARDT MOLL, D.D. With a new Metrical Version of the Psalms, and Philological Notes, by T. J. CONANT, D.D.
10. **Proverbs.** By Prof OTTO ZÖCKLER, D.D. **Ecclesiastes.** By Prof. O. ZÖCKLER, D.D. With Additions, and a new Metrical Version, by Prof. TAYLER LEWIS, D.D. **The Song of Solomon.** By Prof. O. ZÖCKLER, D.D.
11. **Isaiah.** By C. W. E. NAEGELSBACH.
12. **Jeremiah.** By C. W. E. NAEGELSBACH, D.D. **Lamentations.** By C. W. E NAEGELSBACH, D.D.
13. **Ezekiel.** By F W. SCHRÖDER, D.D. **Daniel.** By Professor ZOCKLER, D.D.
14. **The Minor Prophets.** Hosea, Joel, and Amos. By OTTO SCHMOLLER, Ph.D. Obadiah and Micah. By Rev. PAUL KLEINERT. Jonah, Nahum, Habakkuk, and Zephaniah. By Rev. PAUL KLEINERT. Haggai. By Rev. JAMES E. M'CURDY. Zechariah. By T. W. CHAMBERS, D.D. Malachi. By JOSEPH PACKARD, D.D

The Apocrypha. *(Just published.)* By E. C. BISSELL, D.D. One Volume.

NEW TESTAMENT—10 VOLUMES.

1. **Matthew.** With a General Introduction to the New Testament. By J. P. LANGE, D.D. Translated, with Additions, by PHILIP SCHAFF, D.D.
2. **Mark.** By J. P. LANGE, D.D. **Luke.** By J. J. VAN OOSTERZEE.
3. **John.** By J. P. LANGE, D.D.
4. **Acts.** By G. V. LECHLER, D.D., and Rev. CHARLES GEROK.
5. **Romans.** By J. P. LANGE, D.D., and Rev. F. R. FAY.
6. **Corinthians.** By CHRISTIAN F. KLING.
7. **Galatians.** By OTTO SCHMOLLER, Ph.D. **Ephesians and Colossians.** By KARL BRAUNE, D.D. **Philippians.** By KARL BRAUNE, D.D.
8. **Thessalonians.** By Drs. AUBERLEN and RIGGENBACH. **Timothy.** By J. J. VAN OOSTERZEE, D.D. **Titus.** By J. J. VAN OOSTERZEE, D.D. **Philemon.** By J. J. VAN OOSTERZEE, D.D. **Hebrews.** By KARL B. MOLL, D.D.
9. **James.** By J. P. LANGE, D.D., and J. J. VAN OOSTERZEE, D.D. **Peter and Jude.** By G. F. C. FRONMÜLLER, Ph.D. **John.** By KARL BRAUNE, D.D.
10. **The Revelation of John.** By Dr. J. P. LANGE. Together with double Alphabetical Index to all the Ten Volumes on the New Testament, by JOHN H. WOODS.

T. and T. Clark's Publications.

In Twenty handsome 8vo Volumes, Subscription price £5, 5s.,

MEYER'S
COMMENTARY ON THE NEW TESTAMENT.

'Meyer has been long and well known to scholars as one of the very ablest of the German expositors of the New Testament. We are not sure whether we ought not to say that he is unrivalled as an interpreter of the grammatical and historical meaning of the sacred writers. The Publishers have now rendered another seasonable and important service to English students in producing this translation.'—*Guardian.*

(Yearly Issue of Four Volumes, 21s.)
Each Volume will be sold separately at 10s. 6d. to Non-Subscribers.

CRITICAL AND EXEGETICAL
COMMENTARY ON THE NEW TESTAMENT.
ST. MATTHEW'S GOSPEL TO JUDE.

By Dr. H. A. W. MEYER,
OBERCONSISTORIALRATH, HANNOVER.

First Year.—Romans, Two Volumes; Galatians, One Volume; St. John's Gospel, Vol. I. **Second Year.**—St. John's Gospel, Vol. II.; Philippians and Colossians, One Volume; Acts of the Apostles, Vol. I.; Corinthians, Vol. I. **Third Year.**—Acts of the Apostles, Vol. II.; St. Matthew's Gospel, Two Volumes; Corinthians, Vol. II. **Fourth Year.**—Mark and Luke, Two Volumes; Ephesians and Philemon, One Volume; Thessalonians, One Volume (*Dr. Lünemann*). **Fifth Year.**—Timothy and Titus, One Volume (*Dr. Huther*); Peter and Jude, One Volume (*Dr. Huther*); Hebrews, One Volume (*Dr. Lünemann*); James and John, One Volume (*Dr. Huther*).

The series, as written by Meyer himself, is completed by the publication of Ephesians with Philemon in one volume. But to this the Publishers have thought it right to add Thessalonians and Hebrews, by Dr. Lünemann, and the Pastoral and Catholic Epistles, by Dr. Huther.

'I need hardly add that the last edition of the accurate, perspicuous, and learned commentary of Dr. Meyer has been most carefully consulted throughout; and I must again, as in the preface to the Galatians, avow my great obligations to the acumen and scholarship of the learned editor.'—BISHOP ELLICOTT *in Preface to his 'Commentary on Ephesians.'*

'The ablest grammatical exegete of the age.'—PHILIP SCHAFF, D.D.

'In accuracy of scholarship and freedom from prejudice, he is equalled by few.'—*Literary Churchman.*

'We have only to repeat that it remains, of its own kind, the very best commentary of the New Testament which we possess.'—*Church Bells.*

'No exegetical work is on the whole more valuable, or stands in higher public esteem. As a critic he is candid and cautious; exact to minuteness in philology; a master of the grammatical and historical method of interpretation.'—*Princeton Review.*

LOTZE'S MICROCOSMUS.

Just published, in Two Vols., 8vo (1450 pages), price 36s.,

MICROCOSMUS:
CONCERNING MAN AND HIS RELATION TO THE WORLD.
By HERMANN LOTZE.

CONTENTS:—Book 1. The Body. II. The Soul. III. Life. IV. Man. V. Mind. VI. The Microcosmic Order; or, The Course of Human Life. VII. History. VIII. Progress. IX. The Unity of Things.

'These are indeed two masterly volumes, vigorous in intellectual power, and translated with rare ability. . . . This work will doubtless find a place on the shelves of all the foremost thinkers and students of modern times.'—*Evangelical Magazine.*

Just published, in ex. 8vo, price 9s.,

THE OLDEST CHURCH MANUAL
CALLED THE
Teaching of the Twelve Apostles.

The Didachè and Kindred Documents in the Original, with Translations and Discussions of Post-Apostolic Teaching, Baptism, Worship, and Discipline, and with Illustrations and Fac-Similes of the Jerusalem Manuscript.

By PHILIP SCHAFF, D.D., LL.D.

'This is *par excellence* the edition to possess.'—*Freeman.*

'This is by far the most complete *apparatus criticus* for the study of that interesting and important document.'—*British Quarterly Review.*

Just published, in One Vol., 8vo (640 pp.), price 15s.,

HISTORY OF THE SACRED SCRIPTURES OF THE NEW TESTAMENT.
By PROFESSOR E. REUSS, D.D.
Translated from the Fifth Revised and Enlarged Edition.

'One of the most valuable of Messrs. Clark's valuable publications. . . . Its usefulness is attested by undiminished vitality. . . . His method is admirable, and he unites German exhaustiveness with French lucidity and brilliancy of expression. . . . The sketch of the great exegetic epochs, their chief characteristics, and the critical estimates of the most eminent writers, is given by the author with a compression and a mastery that have never been surpassed.'—Archdeacon FARRAR.

www.ingramcontent.com/pod-product-compliance
Lightning Source LLC
Chambersburg PA
CBHW020114170426
43199CB00009B/523